GET BEYOND

YOUR TROUBLED

PAST

You're Not Looking For A Job,
You're Looking For A Person

Date: 3/14/17

GET BEYOND

YOUR TROUBLED

PAST

You're Not Looking For A Job,
You're Looking For A Person

By
John Jeffrey Lundell

First Edition published March 2015

Printed by CreateSpace

Printed in the United States of America

Designed by Kevin Vain, KDV Design & Associates, LLC

ISBN-13: 978-1507778623
ISBN-10: 1507778627

Contents

Preface

Why I Wrote This Book

Get Beyond Your Troubled Past has roots that go back many years, to a time before the Digital Revolution. Although I had no way of knowing it during those early years, my working experiences immediately after graduating from college would prove an invaluable comparison point some thirty years later. I couldn't have imagined the journey that would take me away from the not-for-profit world of education and workforce development to a twenty-six year "diversion" into the private sector and front-line management, only to return to the same line of work now playing out in a vastly different employment landscape.

Gone was the post WWII manufacturing-based economy. In its place was a technology driven, service oriented one, evolving at a rate unimaginable during the 70s. And yet, when it came to the background-challenged person re-entering the workforce, there was something that had not changed—the need to connect with people. In those early years, working as an employment counselor for CETA (a massive, federally funded workforce training and employment program), career success depended heavily on one's ability to directly interact, largely on a face-to-face level. Even though person-to-person contact remained vitally important, a shift was taking place from "finding" to "being found" when it came to making initial contact with prospective employers. This shift, driven largely by technology and digits, was turning many of the tried-and-true methods of job searching, upside down.

This was the state of things as I re-connected with workforce development in the spring of 2008, assisting Nevada Department of Correction inmates searching for work-release jobs. But, there was soon to be a major twist to the story. In a matter of months, the Great Recession clobbered the economy and the employment situation for all workers suddenly took a major turn for the worse. Needless to say, those with significant background problems (such as the inmates I helped daily) were in for a real struggle.

The meltdown of the real estate market and the economy in general (especially in Las Vegas) was the undeniable Big Event. Soon, unemployment skyrocketed and stories of laid-off workers applying for hundreds of jobs and sending out tons of résumés, flooded the media. The shortcomings of the digitally based "new job search" were on full display.

The situation was crystal clear to me. If a background-challenged seeker was to have a shot at success, they would need a different approach.

I developed a method built around two critical concepts:

- Digits are no friend to the background-challenged job seeker.

- Use of a strategy that is **not dependent** upon the digit, can and will work.

This approach didn't just work, it really worked, and it continues to do so. The methodology I developed helping inmates and, in the years that followed, homeless and recovering clients re-entering the workforce, is what this book is about. Anyone with background snags and an inconsistent work history, for any reason, can use it effectively.

It's a success story not without irony. How interesting that lessons in people skills, rooted in a time well before cell phones and personal computers, would turn out to be just what's needed to counteract limits created by all things digital. Yet, that's exactly what I found.

The purpose of this book is to share what has worked for me and my clients, some of whom you'll meet in the pages ahead. I hope you enjoy the book, and I'd love to know what you think. Please share your comments, ideas, and stories by visiting my website.

Travel Well.

John Jeffrey Lundell

www.getbeyonditall.com

October, 2014

Las Vegas, Nevada

"There is nothing new except what has been forgotten."

Marie Antoinette

Introduction

The square shaped envelope slipped out from the pile of mostly junk mail, landing at the edge of my desk. I sorted through and chucked out what remained, then picked up the card and examined the front. The return address read, *M. R. Auttenberg, 3001 Golf Springs Rd., Laviston, MS 38999*. It was December 17th so this was obviously a holiday card, but Auttenberg ... MS ... I drew a total blank.

I opened it. A quaint, Nativity manger scene, a bright yellow long-tailed star, and a bold glittery *Merry Christmas* met my eyes. I flipped the card open and a picture of a man sitting in what looked like a backward lawn swing fell out. He sported a full beard and a broad smile. A New York Yankee baseball cap cocked slightly to the right, sat on his head. He looked relaxed, sitting back on the swing, left leg half crossing his right, arms outstretched across the top of the swing-back. There was no change to my state of total blankness.

Who is this guy?

I skipped the verse and went to the handwritten note on the inside left.

Merry Christmas John!

It's been a while; hope you're doing well. Check out the picture. I decided to grow a beard for Christmas; it's too hot and muggy in the summer ... what do you think? Sort of like Grizzly Adams, right? Anyway, John, I'm doing just fine down here in Mississippi. Don't know if you remember me talking about heading back South—well, I did it.

A glimmer of recognition tickled me, but I still couldn't put the pieces together. I looked at the picture again. Zip, nothing. Yet ... I read on.

John, I've had time to think and reflect, and I have to say I am so Blessed. It's peaceful down here, and I can't thank you enough for guiding me through the last leg of my journey. I got a job with the county, which I really like. It took a while, but I was patient and used your approach. It all panned out. Best of all, I just celebrated eleven years clean and sober. I start each day with my own Personal Job One mantra, and I thank you for that as well.

God Bless and Merry Christmas.

McArthur Reginald (Reggie) Auttenburg

Reggie! Of course ... Reggie Auttenburg, the man with a name no one could forget but a bearded face I couldn't place. Wow, what an unexpected treat. It happens like this. People come into my life and then move on because that's the goal, to help people get back on track and move on with their lives.

The approach Reggie referred to is what you'll learn about in this book, step by step. Chapter One reviews how the microchip has changed the world of work and looking for work. You'll find out what this means for you, a background-challenged individual. What's more, you'll come to understand the twin concepts of Free Agency and the Marketplace and why they're so important for you to know.

Chapter Two focuses on your relationship with reality. Barriers to your success come in two forms, intangible (which are non-real and exist in your mind) and tangible barriers (which are real and exist outside of you). The solution to overcoming intangible barriers, the subject of this chapter, is about awakening to the present moment and living in the now. You'll discover how this works as well as what Reggie wrote about, your Personal Job One. It's a concept of vital importance when it comes to avoiding complete life and job search derailments and implosions.

From awakening and staying present, Chapter Three moves our discussion toward the more hands-on topics of planning, goal setting, and managing your other life priorities. Here, another set of fundamental concepts is introduced, the Five-year Plan and your Job Search Objective. You'll learn how to "reverse engineer" your master plan, to create an entry point, and a personalized Job Search Objective. But, unlike so many "how to" job search systems, my planning and objective setting doesn't take place in a vacuum, as if nothing else were happening in your life. There's a balancing act that must take place, and you'll find out how to forge a collaborative alliance with someone close to insure all life priorities are considered while you work on your job-search plan.

Chapter Four begins with a discussion of the difference between being proactive and reactive and shows you why, in no uncertain terms, being proactive is a must. You'll see how proactivity is used, in a realistic, step-by-step manner, to clean-up neglected, hanging "old business." Also included is an unconventional look at "The System," something you and every other background-challenged person has encountered. Perceptions and attitudes concerning The System are discussed and scrutinized setting the stage for an expanded discussion in the next chapter of the overall mindset you must adopt in order to be successful.

In this introduction, I'm forgetting something that makes this book unique, the characters. For the most part, this is a "how to" book, and I must be honest, I've read a lot of "how to" books over the years. Frequently, I'm bored with them. Too often, they're dry information dumps and system outlines that are helpful and well intentioned, but make for bland reading. There's no one you can identify with or picture actually doing what the book discusses doing. So, I've included Roger, Michael, Catherine, and Walter. Their names have been changed but they're real as can be and represent actual clients I've helped. I hope their stories make this book easier to read and more realistic for you.

In Chapter Five, the notions of your Personal Starting Point and Strategic Acceptance are introduced and reviewed. Finding your true beginning point and learning to accept things as they really are, provide a foundation for the chapter's mindset overview. You will come to know how fairness, truthfulness, and honesty intertwine with integrity, a characteristic critical to building a marketing and sales-based job search model, unique *to* **you!**

The all-important topic of communication skills is the subject of Chapter Six, and you'll be reminded through examples, of how all communication requires the use of one or more of our five senses. Additionally, you'll come to understand with renewed appreciation, it isn't what you intend to communicate that matters but what is received by the other person that truly counts. The review of communication leads naturally to people skills, which, in short, is the critical ability to get along with others.

Rounding out Chapter Six is the relatively new addition to the category of communication, social media. Once you've finished reading this section, you'll understand why a "less is more" approach to social media applies to you and your situation. You'll come away with the know-how to proactively take on this thorny area to your best advantage.

Chapter Seven covers a lot of ground in preparation for the beginning of your actual job search. The development of and need for your personal narrative is presented. From your narrative, you're shown how to create your unique "Delivering The Mail" statement, the actual words and phrases you'll use to honestly describe your background issue in concise, deliberate terms. Next, you'll learn how and why to conduct your own background check, followed by a discussion of job applications and résumés. Learning how to compile and complete both is just the beginning. You'll also discover why it's essential to see job applications and résumés for what they are, elimination tools.

Arriving at Chapter Eight means you are truly getting down to business. All the preceding information and preparation will finally make sense and drop into place. This is where the search for your first job is plotted out using your Job Search Objective. This Objective will align with your Five-year Plan and Goal, and you'll be coached in how to implement your search using a seven-step marketing and sales approach. Critical to this chapter (and not to be missed) is a discussion of where not to look, a topic skipped over by many job searchers. The chapter concludes with a step-by-step explanation of how to Deliver The Mail, your presentation of the condensed version of your personal narrative, which is your background challenge.

Next comes learning how to retain your first job. Chapter Nine presents the four stages of a first position which dovetails in the later stage with a deliberate move to job number two, all part of your unfolding Five-year Plan. It's not easy to maintain your current job while actively pursuing your next one, but the best ways to accomplish this are discussed in detail.

One of the by-products of securing and retaining your initial job is the creation of a platform, which will be used and leveraged as you move forward. This is the subject of Chapter Ten. The explanation of targeted networking and building of people-links will bring the meaning of this book's subtitle, You're Not Looking for a Job, You're Looking for a Person, into clear view. You'll come away knowing why relationship building, in the context of positioning yourself for advancement, is the key to your continued success.

Chapter Eleven explains how best to use the contact information you'll gradually generate, and also provides you with examples of how to set up your own contact management system. You'll learn the difference between contacts and people-links and how to connect the relationship links you develop over time to neutralize and eliminate the barriers that exist as a result of your background problem.

The final chapter takes you back again to where you started as you finish reading the book, planning. Chapter Twelve outlines a series of specific reasons why a Master Plan is crucially important and what it can do for you. The chapter ends with a quick review of the book's key concepts and a motivational passage written to inspire, challenge, and encourage you to create your Five-year Plan and take on your Big Goal.

Yes, there is a positive, exciting career out there for you as a person with background issues. This book is unique because most books on job-hunting only mention people with stellar, perfect pasts, not the twenty-five percent of the population who've experienced some of the slings and arrows of life. Follow the steps, stay focused, and you will arrive at your goal.

Welcome aboard, it's time to get to work.

Chapter One

The Situation on the Ground

The world of work has changed a great deal over the last thirty years when the term "service economy" first made its way to mainstream America. By 2010, the service sector accounted for two thirds of the economic output and seven out of ten jobs in the US. This is a big change from 1950 when three fifths of the economic output and half of all jobs were connected to the production of goods.

"What does this have to do with me?" you may ask. "Who cares how it's changed? My concern is dealing with things as they are now. I got a lousy work history and a record; how am I supposed to get anywhere in this or any other economy?"

Trust me when I say it should mean a lot to you. For starters, there is no fixed "right now" economically. The work world is in flux in a large part due to the microchip and automation. Whether you realize it or not, you're a Free Agent worker competing with everyone else in the Marketplace. We'll cover this and much more in Chapter One but, first, I'd like to introduce you to Roger.

Roger: from One Relapse to Another

I received Albert's call a little after ten on a Friday morning.

"John, Roger's had a setback," Albert's tone was dry and to the point. Roger was a new client and Albert was his Alcoholics Anonymous sponsor. From a job search and re-entry perspective, there was no "setback" because the process hadn't started for Roger yet.

"What happened?" I had an idea but forced the thought from my mind.

"Well, he spent most of Wednesday at O'Reilly's Pub. Guess I don't have to paint a picture how that went ...." Albert sighed audibly. "At least he had the presence of mind to call his sister so no driving was involved, thank God. Anyway, I talked with him yesterday. He's frustrated and angry with himself. He's embarrassed too, especially after our meeting last week."

I met Albert at a networking breakfast a month earlier where I spoke about job search challenges faced by people with background issues. Albert took the initiative, arranging an appointment for both he and Roger at my office. The meeting went well. Albert, in recovery from alcoholism for nearly 20 years and an experienced AA sponsor, didn't mess around. He quickly handed the ball off to Roger then stepped outside for a cup of coffee as the two of us got acquainted.

Roger said he was tired of his long battle with alcohol and drugs and was ready to get back on track. I gave him homework assignments to complete and scheduled our first working appointment.

Roger's a fortunate guy because Albert's a decent, caring person. What's more, Albert's willing to take action. For this, Roger can be doubly thankful because when it comes to seeking out assistance with employment re-entry, it's rarely the person with the problem who steps up. Stating this clearly, in the best of all situations it would be **YOU** (a background-challenged person) who pulls this book from the shelf or finds it online, but it usually isn't. Instead, it's an Albert, someone's spouse, sister, brother, business associate, or helping professional who takes the horse by the reins and gets things moving.

I care deeply about my clients. After helping many people over the years with background issues when it comes to getting a job, I have a great deal of compassion for people viewed by many as "unemployable." However, I'm a realist. I have to stay in a strong place of "tough love" with them because, over time, I've discovered that approach works best to help people make positive changes and become a functioning part of society again. I call it "Compassionate Tough Love" or CTL.

Most of us have a vague idea how "interventions" work. For example, when a family takes intervening steps to help a loved one mired deep in substance abuse. But interventions (the act of coming in between the usual pattern of events to stop or change something) come in many forms. Generally, interventions have two common characteristics.

- First, interventions occur by way of a person or group of people, not the person in crisis.

- Second, typically, there's an associated next step. For example, an arrest leads to an incarceration, substance abuse leads to treatment, a life crisis leads to counseling, etcetera.

Roger's behavior, which resulted in a relapse, turned into his own personal intervention moment. He called his sister (thankfully) who called his sponsor. Roger got involved on his own behalf by halting his alcohol consumption at Reilly's Pub and making the call. It was up to him to take the next step by showing up prepared for our scheduled meeting.

"So, is he still at his sister's house?" I assumed he was, but needed confirmation.

"Exactly, says he won't go anywhere, and I believe him. He seems pretty shaken right now … I don't know; I hate to see him veer off course, but maybe this will get him focused and back on track."

"Right, it might," I replied. "Okay, we have an appointment this Tuesday. Nothing's changed from my perspective; I still expect him to make it as planned. I guess we'll see if he's ready to actually get down to business."

I thanked Albert for bringing me up to speed, hung up the phone, and thought about Roger. Here he was, a 44-year old man, laying low at his sister's home after what turned out to be a minor relapse. Thank goodness it was minor. But Roger didn't contact me, his sponsor, Albert, did.

During our initial meeting, Roger stated he was ready. But he wasn't, not quite. He was getting ready to get ready. He was still in reactive behavior mode. Albert was correct; Roger needed something to jar him out of his slumber, which is just what happened.

The Work Environment Shakeup

The origin of the Information Age and the Digital Revolution is essential to this book. It's an important topic for people challenged with background issues when it comes to getting a job. Perhaps it's not so important how we got to this point technologically. What's vital to understand is what it means to challenged job seekers. In short, it has changed the job-hunting game forever. To quote American economist and George Mason University professor Tyler Cowen, "Everything that can be measured, rated, graded, and categorized, will be." In other words, the digit makes it possible and relatively easy to quantify and analyze information about you without having to actually meet you. This is a problem.

The Digital Age gradually came into existence beginning in the late 1950s to the late 1970s with the tectonic plate shift from analog to digital technology. The 1980s saw the rise of personal computers and, in the 1990s, cell phones and Internet use exploded on the scene. The 2000s gave us texting and HDTVs, and the 2010s ushered in social media advancements and cloud computing. These are easy tip-of-the-iceberg examples of how the Digital Revolution has impacted daily life. Clearly, we're at the cusp of an economic and societal paradigm shift on the order of the Industrial Revolution.

One of the critical offshoots of the switch from analog to digitally based communication and information storage is the creation and explosion of databases containing massive amounts of personal information. Back in the day (pre-1980), the amount of stored personal information was a fraction of what's available today. It was difficult to share data with users out of immediate proximity to the storage location.

With the move to a digital base, combined with the internet, the faucet has been cranked wide open. As recent high-profile personal information security breaches at national retailers and other highly respected businesses have shown, the digits are frequently out in front of the controls set in place to manage their awesome capabilities. These high-tech examples of information leaks are alarming. Yet, in spite of investigations and proposed regulations to address this growing problem, the shift toward more omni-available information of all types marches on. The toothpaste is out of the tube.

Vendors of every stripe keep springing up, exploiting opportunities to offer information-based products to a continually growing list of customers. Spirited competition and leapfrogging technological advances work to the benefit of buyers and users of this information, including employers. Service packages are marketed and tailored for checking criminal history, driving records, past employment, military records, educational certificates, and degrees, not to mention credit history, and a wide variety of publicly available information that was formerly confidential.

Why is this important to a job seeker with background concerns? It's simple, because information about you is now cheap and easier than ever to obtain. This should come as no surprise but, frankly, many people pretend otherwise. All too often, people with background problems look for ways to hide out, rather than manage and get on top of these problems. Others grapple with background snags by creating their own versions of reality, trying to spin the issues away. Still others state no problems exist, either by sticking their heads in the sand or by simply lying to prospective employers.

The digits have you in a vice grip. To a degree, they have **everyone** nailed to the wall.

You need a way around, a means of offsetting the here-to-stay reality of easy-to-access information about anyone's background. Perhaps "a way around" isn't the ideal expression here, but it serves its purpose. There's a critical need to develop an alternative route leading to gainful employment.

My experience has shown that the best route is found by connecting and networking with other people—yes, actual living, breathing, human beings. Of course, this is exactly what many background-challenged folks don't want. To many, the natural thing is to avoid direct contact with other people as much as possible. For example:

- *"It's better not to get into it, right?"* Wrong.

- *"Bringing all that up will eliminate me from the running, for sure. So, what do I have to lose anyway, right?"* Wrong again.

- *"No way I'm gonna check off that I have a felony. It's better just to take my chances they won't find out, right?"* Way wrong.

This book isn't about the Digital Revolution. It's about the **why** and **how** of being a background-challenged person dealing with the new digital reality **and** how working directly with others is the best way to win.

Get Beyond Your Troubled Past and the approach I'll share on these pages was written specifically for you, the ex-offender, recovering addict, or mental health patient trying to compete in the Marketplace.

Although each reader is a unique individual with their own personal story of hardship, from the perspective of employers looking for the right person to fit into his or her organization, you'll frequently be seen as a liability. Why? Because your life situation and chopped-up work history, represents complications unattractive to many employers. Plus, you're easier to spot than ever, thanks to the tools of the digital Information Age, so readily available and effortless to implement in their human resources operations. But don't despair; your challenges can be overcome.

As the Information Age hurtles forward, based on years of experience helping good people in this predicament, I know the best approach for those challenged by background concerns begins by stepping off to the sidelines, to reflect and re-group. Yes, the realities of our new digital world have made things complicated and more difficult. Yet, there's a way to address your concerns by using an objective-based, personal interaction approach to get back in the workforce.

Get Beyond Your Troubled Past wasn't written to address every set of circumstances. How could it? Instead, I suggest you look for what is applicable to your situation and the specific challenges you face. Absorb those ideas relevant to you, using a flexible, adaptable mindset.

Let me restate what I said earlier about the necessity to meet and work directly with people. It's critical for you. In fact, you can look at it from this perspective: unlike the average "Joe Job Seeker," you won't find much success by just looking for a job like everyone else.

- You won't get hired by a business.

- A company won't offer you a position.

- Joe might get a job this way, but not you.

In your case, you don't want to look for **a job**. You're looking for **a person**. Getting hired by a business or company implies going through human resources departments and hierarchy with ironclad systems and procedures in place. These entities **hate** the kinds of challenges you represent. They will work to avoid them, which means, they want to **avoid you**.

There's a great deal of valuable and very usable information presented in the upcoming pages, including plenty of strategies and lots of shared techniques. But honestly, none of it is rocket science. On the contrary, I want your feet firmly planted on the ground. I'll present these proven strategies in a straightforward, realistic, easy-to-follow manner. But strategies and techniques aside, to maximize your odds of success, plan on working with and through other people—to get the job and to keep it.

You Are a Free Agent

For many people, when they hear the term "free agent" the world of professional sports comes to mind. If not pro sports, some other profession or vocation equally far-removed from their daily lives is summoned up. Most of us don't consider ourselves, or our relationship to the world of work, in this way.

For the most part, we're social beings gravitating to groups where we'll find like-minded people. Contributing to this tendency are thousands of years of shared human experience. Humankind has arrived in the twenty-first century, not by going it alone, but by working together. Most people seek the structure, order, and security associated with groups, over the wide-open frontier of opportunities possible when we choose to go it alone.

But the world is changing. The realities of the last century are not those of this new century. Globalization has arrived. The U.S. economy, and the nature of work, is evolving. The Digital Revolution, coupled with shocking events including the collapse of the Internet Bubble, 9/11, and, more recently, the Great Recession, all share one common element—disruption to what we've always known.

The result to the American workforce has been profound. Concerns over the loss of old-line manufacturing jobs has given way to worries over losses in the new service economy. Entire job classifications have disappeared due to outsourcing, automation, and digitization. Real wages have decreased over the last three decades as the cost of health care and other benefits have steadily transferred from employer to employee.

It's a very different, fast evolving world of work today compared to the last century. According to the Bureau of Labor Statistics, in January of 2012 the median number of years workers stayed with their current employer was about 4.6 years in total. For workers aged 25-34, the average years worked was 3.2 years. For those workers 18-30, years of employment dropped to approximately two years.

These statistics provide the basis for the **first reason** you should see yourself as a Free Agent. More and more American workers (especially younger people) are or will experience free agency in their work life.

Two facts jump out regarding the data above and the overall employment situation. First is the trend. The length of time people are working with a particular employer known as "tenure" when compared to the beginning of the Digital Revolution, is declining. Second, large chunks of the American workforce are not prepared for, equipped, or even capable of managing a successful career as a Free Agent worker. I'm referring to everyone in the work force, not just those with background snags. This is the direction the working landscape is headed.

Where does this leave the background-challenged worker? The answer, sadly, is at the end of the line unless you take disruption-busting action, which is the purpose of this book.

There's an important distinction to make here, I encourage you to choose Free Agent status rather than becoming a reluctant Free Agent. The truth is, you already are one because you're taking responsibility for your career and control over your destiny. When you identify with free agency, it's easier to stay heads-up and awake to what's happening as a worker. This is the **second reason** you'll benefit from seeing yourself this way; it makes you a far more effective employee. You understand your business is about providing A1 Service for your employer, who's actually your customer. The fact that you understand this will be demonstrated each day on the job. Believe me, it will be noticed.

Back to the distinction of choosing to see yourself this way in order to avoid being forced into a free agency situation not of your choosing. Each time a background-challenged person checks out and then attempts to jump back into the workforce (something independent workers do continually) the entire hiring process starts fresh. Here's where the "back of the line" comment fits in. With your background blemishes, you'll be considered last. There will always be one other person in line for a position who is like you in every way, except they aren't burdened with background issues. So, here's the memo—see and perform as if you're a Free Agent in order to decrease your chances of actually having to be a Free Agent.

The **third reason** to embrace the idea of free agency is it provides a fresh, positive mental framework for your job search. It's much easier to see yourself as being in charge of the search process, rather than as a person standing around hat in hand, begging. If you approach it as a Free Agent, you're not begging.

The **fourth reason** is it will prevent you from settling in and getting too comfortable once you gain employment. Recall again the Bureau of Labor statistics. You may be fortunate and find a mutually beneficial fit, remaining with an employer for an extended period of time. This could be great for you. But the statistics counsel job-hunters to think differently now. They reveal your Free Agent wagon train will soon be back on the trail. You're wise to keep your saw sharp and your head up. Staying ready, slightly on edge, and engaged in your work will help keep you there. When it's time to move on, you'll be ready, because that's what Free Agents occasionally do. Anyway, it's part of your plan, which we'll cover in Chapter Two.

Taking on a Free Agent persona means you'll rarely stand still. There are many people who settle in and stop moving only to find themselves unemployed and completely unprepared for the reality of the current economic state of affairs. Don't let this happen to you, especially you. The four reasons above are why cultivating a Free Agent mindset is a smart way to go.

Begin by accepting the fact that you are, and always will be, essentially a Free Agent, independently making your way in the Marketplace. Weave this into your job search by being proactive, methodical, and persistent. Know that once employed, you're in the business of providing service. You're being paid to produce results. Approaching your working life in this manner will allow you to compete effectively with everyone else regardless of the background situation.

The bottom line is you must see yourself as being in business for yourself. Not necessarily the same as someone who owns a brick and mortar or storefront business, but you're doing your own thing nonetheless. This creates a higher degree of responsibility, buy-in, and a sense of ownership in your work right off the bat. Seeing yourself as being a self-directed Free Agent provides a flexible, portable platform, allowing you to take your "Business Owner Mindset" anywhere and to anyone, in order to achieve your goals.

The Marketplace

Where is your success as a Free Agent job seeker determined? When I ask this question, the usual response is to ask a question in return for clarification. What exactly do I mean by, "*Where*?" Is it possible I really mean, "By whom?" Perhaps I'm fishing for my client to announce, "I determine my own success."

Without additional prompting, most people eventually answer their success is determined by:

- Their employer

- Themselves

- The economy

- Their education

- The HR department

- The level of competition

- Globalization and free trade

- Discrimination, and so on

It's all over the map. Generally, the responses focus on specifics and details. In economic terms, the micro verses the macro point of view.

Of course, in a general sense, none of these answers are flatly incorrect, there are many things that determine whether or not a job seeker will experience success. But the "where" of my question is missed and this achieves my objective. These micro answers are an indication of the job seeker's perspective—the trees and not the forest. Unrecognized is the field of play where all decisions are really made.

The "where" I'm referencing is conceptual, not tangible. It's a place and a thing combined. Still, we can't see, hear, smell, touch, or taste it directly. There are rules and ways of behaving associated with it. And, like the thing itself, these rules are abstract and hard to pin down.

Most people accept the existence of this place/thing but find the essence of it hard to grasp because there's no easy way to measure, value, or compare it—other than results. It operates 24/7, non-stop. It's ahead of, behind, and all around each of us. It's where all business happens.

It's the **Marketplace**.

To find out what it is and how it functions, you must enter the Marketplace and experience it directly. But here's the problem with most job seekers' encounters, they're of the "plunge right in" type. Little, if any, thought is given to where and how things play out. There's no assessment taken from 30,000 feet. Instead, job seekers drop to three feet and are unable to appreciate the lay of the land, finding themselves surrounded by nothing but grass, bushes, and trees.

Taking a micro view such as this creates a problem. Humans are programmed to see things in terms of polarity, as good or bad, right or wrong, fair or unfair. But the Marketplace doesn't operate this way. It doesn't care that we want to size it up or figure it out. It doesn't care that we want to take a class on it, with Cliff Notes, quizzes, and groups meetings to kick it around. Our need to have someone tell us what it's about and perhaps hold our hand as we enter it, is of absolutely no concern to the Marketplace.

As a job seeker and eventual Free Agent seller of service, you must embrace the concept of the Marketplace and see yourself as a participant. You need come to terms with the fact that the Marketplace has no emotions or opinions. You must understand it just doesn't care who's on the field and who wins or loses. Getting your head around the fact that the dispassionate Marketplace is both *the location where the game takes place* and *the game itself* is essential.

If the first half of a successful job search comes from seeing yourself as a Free Agent, then accepting and understanding the concept of the Marketplace is the other half. Absorbing and integrating both concepts allows you, as the job seeker, to take to the field as an actual participant and not a reactive wannabe pretender. Instead of feeling trapped and hemmed in by all you don't see or understand, you begin to experience freedom, because you **know** you're a Free Agent and you **know** you're operating within the Marketplace.

Coming to this point of integration requires you to abandon excuses and blame. Without them you're better able to see yourself for what you really are, a seller of a service operating within an open forum, devoid of attributes like fairness, equality, and goodness. It's not to say these things don't exist, but you must be prepared to function without them.

As people, we're incapable of total objectivity. Nevertheless, the Free Agent job seeker must work toward it, cutting loose the constraints of assigning decision power to anyone or anything. Sure, you didn't get the position because the owner's brother-in-law was selected out of nowhere or the manager picked someone with the same cultural or ethnic background. You're frustrated, angry, and resentful because it's not fair or right.

Let's pretend for a moment that the Marketplace had a point of view. If so, it might say you don't understand the rules of this specific game; that brothers-in-law are always picked over non-brothers-in-law or that managers never pick candidates from outside their own social group or ethnicity. If the Marketplace could communicate with you directly, it would tell you not to spend time and energy stewing on any of this. Instead, learn from this reality. Take it in stride and move on. Furthermore, it would remind you that your Job Search Objective, covered in Chapter Three, hasn't yet been achieved and that any time or energy spent on these outcomes is wasted and fruitless. You would be told bluntly that the Marketplace couldn't care less about your feelings. You're merely a player who wins, loses, or draws.

All this is cold and harsh, but true. As an independent Free Agent, focus on that which you have some possibility of managing—your side of the equation. You have no control over the Marketplace. You can however *exert influence* as you participate. To do this, you must see things accurately and objectively. You must be open, willing, and teachable. The Marketplace provides everyone with a continual stream of lessons. Are **you** ready and willing to listen? Are **you** up to making the adjustments necessary to achieve your objective?

In my experience, of the two concepts including Free Agency and the Marketplace, the Marketplace is the concept background-challenged individuals have the most trouble embracing. Background issues rarely exist in a vacuum. Frequently, they're outward manifestations of inner baggage, emotional scar tissue, pain, grief, and fear. Thus, it's too easy for someone with these constraints to lay blame, project frustration, wallow, and complain. If the Marketplace could speak to you, it would say:

I don't care, because I can't care. I'm not capable or programmed to care. I set up the game and report the results. It's your job to compete, bring your best game, advancing from a win and learning from a loss. You do with it what you will.

In the end, Free Agents accept the Marketplace for what it is. With this acceptance comes the possibility of achieving success, quicker and more fully than otherwise would be the case. Acceptance and adjustment leads to freedom, but at a price—responsibility. Being in charge of your future is no small thing.

The Wrap-up

My intention is for you to understand there are few safe harbors other than those you arrange for yourself. Your assignment for this chapter is to think back to how you missed the fact you've always been a Free Agent.

- How you expected or assumed others would pave the way, but didn't ….

- How you were clueless about the rules of the Marketplace and, in the process, blindsided by a work situation that could have been avoided, but wasn't ….

But don't take this as license for a pity party. No way. I want you to *get real* about how things actually work. As you'll see in Chapter Two, we'll spend little time mulling over the past. For now, think how things might have gone differently if you operated with a Free Agent mindset and some understanding of the rules-of-the-road in the Marketplace.

Action Steps

See yourself being a Free Agent.

Imagine being a third person observer, watching <u>you</u> in the Marketplace.

Chapter Two

Waking Up to Reality

Chapter One painted a broad landscape readying the canvas for additional job search details. The picture is taking shape; however, the backdrop still needs work. Chapter Two will add to our picture by introducing the important concepts of staying present, identifying your Personal Job One, and getting on board. But first, I'd like you to meet Michael.

Michael: Struggling with Voices from the Past

He sat in the chair next to the bookcase just like he did the first time he visited my office many months earlier. Michael was fidgety, both legs tapping to silent music. He fingered the edges of his cap, rolling it around slowly in his right hand.

"Michael, you seem anxious, what's up?" I asked.

"Yeah, well, getting out and 'positioning myself' as you call it, is ... ah, I don't know; its hard man," he glanced up quickly and then returned to fiddling with his cap.

"You've done it before. Remember the first time you came to see me?" I replied, doing my best to encourage him. "Wow, talk about being gun shy, but you did just fine."

Michael looked up, giving me a half-smile. Saying he'd been reluctant was putting it mildly. The first few months were a struggle. Six months out of prison and nothing was working for Michael in the job search department. He picked up a little temporary work, but nothing permanent. The start, stop, and start-over-again cycle got to him. He was frustrated, angry, and in serious need of an attitude adjustment.

"What made the difference then?" I asked Michael. My intent was bringing him back to what worked, what helped him turn the corner before.

"I know ... I know where you're going with this," he said, his eyes averting my gaze.

"What? You know what?" I pressed him.

"I know it's up to me, I mean its attitude stuff and being likeable. I get it, I know. It just seems like it's taking forever," he said meeting my eyes for the first time that day.

"I'd say you're right on track. You just finished year one at Arnie's, with flying colors I might add. According to the plan, it's time to get out and set things in motion for your next gig, right?" We both knew the plan backwards and forwards.

"Right, no, that's the plan for sure."

"So, what's on your mind Michael? Is everything all right at work? Anything I should know about?"

"No, everything's cool at the job, really good actually; it just seems like everything is dragging out," he said.

I took a stab.

"So, how's everything with Victoria?"

"Man, exactly. I mean, that's where it's hard for me, really hard."

It's time for the back story. Michael had a bumpy childhood resulting in an extensive juvenile record. At 21, he picked up a minor drug possession charge and received probation, which he violated. Another arrest for being an accomplice to car and identity theft, along with his probation violation, landed him in prison on a three to five year sentence. He served a little over three years and was released on parole to live with his sister, who, along with their elderly mother, contributed to his support. As part of the arrangement, Michael was required by his sister to attend her church. He did and that's where he met Victoria. Meeting and connecting with her rocked his world in a big way.

But, there was a catch; she wasn't playing his game. She liked him all right, but she wouldn't budge on the deal breakers. If Michael was to have any chance of a future with her, he needed to get and keep his personal and vocational ducks in a row every day. He was doing everything right but he couldn't make the clock move ahead any faster. The plan was the plan, the schedule was the schedule, and both were long-term. Michael didn't fight this, he understood. But, in the meantime, it was killing him with impatience.

"I understand," I empathized. "Are you two still on track, any wavering or mixed messages from her?"

"No, we're good. She's unbelievable. It scares the hell out of me. I mean, what if she decides to change up on me?" he said, his voice cracking slightly. "I couldn't take that, you know what I mean, John?" He brushed back an invisible tear. The fidgeting stopped.

Michael set his cap on the adjacent chair and softly thumped both feet on the floor.

"Here's what I know, Michael. You have a plan, and you're working it. Surprise, surprise, you're one of the most likeable guys working at Arnie's. Who would've predicted that a year and a half ago, right? What's more, you're all over the back of the house, and you like it. Whatever Chef Thomas tosses your way, you nail it every time. But, now it's time to position yourself for the next leg of your journey. I've seen this before. Your success is making you nervous. So is the mere thought of messing up with Victoria. So, what's your next move?"

"My next move is to stick with the plan. I get that. But the pressure is building. I mean it's exciting and scary at the same time."

"And your biggest concern?"

"Well, Victoria. Really, she's incredible ...."

"And, what about your sister and your mom?"

"Yeah, they all want the same thing, for me to stay on track. Me too."

Staying In the Here and Now

Being unemployed and searching for a job can be an emotional minefield, fraught with dangers. For starters, there are ongoing financial concerns to contend with. Bills and payments don't stop arriving just because you're out of work. What's more, your roles don't change; you're still a spouse, a sibling, or a child of someone who may depend on you for financial and emotional support, in part or in full.

Financial concerns can build up, resulting in enormous pressure for job seekers. Job searching itself is demanding and stressful.

When you include the additional stress boosters of how to pay for things, life can become a grueling slog just to get level again.

Given all this, it's no wonder you may have a hard time carrying out a simple job search, not to mention a complex, detailed one. Have you experienced this? Have you tried to maintain your focus and keep your mind clear as the floor slid out from under you and the puzzle parts of your life whirled out away from you in every direction?

A common recommendation given to job seekers is to view the search for a job as **a job itself**. I agree, but there's more to it than this recommendation alone. Dig into this idea a bit and you'll discover that, as a job searcher, you must successfully manage both external and internal components to seeking employment.

When I say "external components" I'm referring to "the doing" of job searching, something we'll get into in detail in the chapters ahead. It means doing everything necessary to look sharp, act sharp, and touch all the bases. It also means carrying out your search in a disciplined, organized, methodical manner. Doing the external components the right way is demanding and requires as much effort and attention as you can bring to the game. This is where most of the "*see it as a job*" advisors focus their attention, on time management, organization, and follow-up.

The "internal components" are harder to pin down. This refers to what's happening in your mind while so much energy is being exerted outwardly. If you could write your own script on the search process, you might start here, by writing your character as a person who's calm and completely clear-of-mind internally, regardless of what's thrown in your direction. That would be nice, but you didn't write the screenplay originally. You'll probably show up on set with whatever frame of mind you have at the moment.

The point is, when it's time to begin, it's time. The first two chapters of *Get Beyond Your Troubled Past* set the stage in preparation for Chapter Three where your actual work begins. Once you start, don't stop. Keep moving forward in a steady and measured way. The process I present is about doing, not dawdling. There's no time to dwell on the past, worry about the future, or fix old, deep-seated problems. From the point of view of the Marketplace, you're either employable or you're not. Period. And the clock is running.

On the outside, you simply manage how you look, how you present yourself, and how you play your cards hand by hand. On the inside, you strive to find the best ways to manage your feelings and emotions because, if the internal components are ignored, you can and probably will sabotage all your diligent external work. That's why, in the best of all worlds, you'd write a script giving yourself the external and internal attributes of a job search rock star. Why not? You'd look good, feel great, and implement everything in slam-dunk fashion. Then again, it might not be so easy. You might see yourself nailing down the external components; however, those pesky internal issues are another matter.

Fortunately, there's a simple fix. It requires a shift within you, a subtle change of perspective. That's all. There's no cost or tools necessary. The shift I'm describing happens internally and instantly by moving into the present moment. When you do this, you begin operating in the here and now. It's simple but, for many people, it's not necessarily easy. Challenges and issues with **past events** deeply rooted inside you have a tendency to surface in unsupportive ways when the pressure ramps up. Worry and anxiety about possible **things yet to come** can magnify and literally stop you dead in your tracks if given full rein and allowed to run amuck.

So, what does it mean to function in the present moment? Consider this. All you really have to work with is the present moment, right now. The past is history and the future is unseen and yet to come. All anyone ever has is right now. When tomorrow comes, it's another present moment. You can pretend otherwise, and your mind will try to convince you it isn't the case. The truth is, we all must do everything we do in the now, the present moment.

Here's the real issue for all job seekers—you need to follow through on your job search plan while managing the usual demands placed on you by family and those close to you. Life continues happening, unfolding predictably some days and unpredictably on other days. It's like you're the actor in an improv sketch and you don't know what's coming your way next. But for you it's not a "sketch" or a "scene," it's your life.

The load's even heavier for background-challenged people like you. Stuff has happened. There are things on file. This is all the more reason for thinking, living, and working in the present. In fact, staying present is more than a mere suggestion or recommendation. It's absolutely essential. Every time you find yourself thinking about what went wrong in the past or worrying about the future, you need to bring your awareness back to the present. It takes work but you can do it. Old, unresolved past issues will find ways to resurface at the worst time. Anxiety and stress about things that haven't happened can drain your energy and take your focus off the ball.

Remember, you're a Free Agent operating in a Marketplace that doesn't care about you or your story. There's freedom in that knowledge, but there's a responsibility, too. So get straight with the way things are for you. Stay present, cutting loose negative stuff from your past and ignoring, for the moment, future things that aren't relevant yet.

The first step in managing all aspects of your life while job searching, is accepting everything is happening all at once. Additionally, the whole experience may be taking you way outside your usual life-pattern and your comfort zone. Your acceptance of what's happening in reality is your highway to operating in the present. Non-acceptance is the opposite, and it won't help you get to your goals, ever. Not accepting reality prevents you from doing what you must do today. It's a mind game leading to inefficiency and ultimately to ineffectiveness. Learn to live in the present, **accept things** now so you can **change things later**.

Your goal is being "on" and fully engaged with what's actually happening to and around you every moment. Being on and engaged means there is no past or future to occupy any part of your mind or body, only what's happening right this instant. For most people, the experience of being and working in the present moment comes as a relief. Gone is baggage hauled aboard long ago. Missing is the stress and fear about unknown things yet to come. This new experience will happen as if you're remembering something you've never learned—something helpful and beneficial that's waited patiently for the right time to surface into your awareness.

Your Personal Job One

This is a book about job search, job retention, and job advancement for people with background challenges. Or, it's a book about people with background challenges who want to know more about searching for jobs, keeping jobs, and advancing in a career. Stating it the first way puts the focus on the search. Stating it the second way places the focus on a person, the background-challenged person and their situation. Let's stay with the second definition because people, like yourself, are important first and foremost, and the job comes after that.

Having a background issue in many ways is like chronic homelessness. It happens as a result of something else. There's always an underlying reason or cause for background problems. All too frequently, the reasons are like the familiar elephant in the room analogy. Everyone can see it but, for whatever reason, they act like the big elephant isn't there. People talk around it, pretending it doesn't exist. Everyone is willing to ignore the obvious and avoid addressing the situation in an honest way.

Using homelessness as an example, no one aspires to become a homeless person. The condition came about due to something else going on in that person's life. Placing a homeless person into a housing situation with little or no regard for what caused the condition in the first place doesn't address the core issues. A roof and a safe, warm, dry place to sleep helps, of course, but it doesn't really fix anything. The underlying issues will soon bubble to the surface again exposing the homeless person's struggle to become self-sufficient.

This example may not apply to everyone with background issues. If you're exempt from underlying issues, well, thank your lucky stars. But, for the sake of those readers grappling with underlying problems, I want to be crystal clear about this point. For you, Job One is not about your job search or your job. It's about shining a spotlight on what might be the base cause of your background problems.

For example, consider the person who's a recovering addict. If this describes you, then your Job One is staying in recovery. Everything else rests upon this. There is no other way to say it, no other way to spin it. The sequence of events must be, first, you get clean and sober. Second, you stay clean and sober. Third, you search for, secure, and retain employment—as a clean and sober person. For you, the priority is and always will be staying in recovery, forever.

I can see you sighing and asking, "But, John, isn't this obvious? How could anyone expect to move ahead if they don't remain clean and sober? It only makes sense, right?"

This isn't a book about recovery. It's a book about how things really work in the world we live in. Again, let's return to the Marketplace, which doesn't care about your addiction, your issues, or the difficulties you've had. The Marketplace also doesn't care about problems you're currently experiencing as a result of an addiction to drugs, alcohol, problem gambling, or any other substance or behavior that doesn't serve you in living a successful, happy life. From the perspective of the Marketplace if you get in and stay in recovery, you have a shot at a functional, successful, happy life. If you don't, your chances plummet, spiraling downward.

The point I'm driving home, perhaps relentlessly, is the Marketplace couldn't care less how life goes for you, me, or anyone else. How you cleaned up, are staying clean, and all the rest, is of no consequence. Either you are or you aren't in recovery and staying there.

The same can be said if you're a person with a criminal record or someone battling a mental health condition that's gotten in the way of sustained employment. You have your own Job One, which is your starting place for putting your life back together again. For an ex-offender it could be about introducing yourself to new places, new people, new things, and, at all costs, avoiding the situations that contributed to your record. If you've been a mental health patient, it could mean staying on your medication and retaining your connections to the counselors and therapists who've helped lead you out of the darkness and into the light again.

Whatever can derail you from getting back on track is your **Personal Job One**, or PJO. Do you know what it is for you? If so, write it down and dedicate yourself to staying on track with your PJO, first and foremost. Whether it's

- Remaining in recovery from drugs, alcohol, gambling, etc.

- Gaining the skills necessary to be self-sufficient and independent

- Avoiding people and situations that could cause recidivism

- Staying on your medication and in touch with your counselor or therapist

You know what you need to do. If you need help with how to do it, reach out to the people and resources who will help you stay on track. When you have identified and written down your PJO and are focused on making it your first priority, then you can start your job search, not before. In most cases, your PJO becomes sort of the elephant in the room. It's probably easy to identify it and write it down, as I suggested above. However, as you know better than anyone else does, it can be very difficult to manage. Even so, recognizing, affirming, and building any relevant PJO into your job search game plan is not an option. If you have a PJO, incorporating it into your long-term plan is essential. In fact, it's so important I'll continue touching on this frequently going forward chapter by chapter.

Grasping the Marketplace point of view that no one cares may seem cold and frustrating, lacking in compassion, and not want you want to read—yet it's the truth. Build your foundation on what's real and what's true in the world. See yourself as a person who is finally the captain of your own ship while operating without blinking in the penetrating sunlight of the present moment.

Getting On Board

I have identified two things associated with achieving long-term results: operating in the present and acknowledging the existence of your PJO. These concepts are vital to what I know is the best approach for you. I believe embracing and implementing them are in your best interest. For those helping background-challenged job seekers find their way, this information is essential to providing the best support and encouragement you possibly can.

I'll be blunt here, because that's one of the things I do best. There's not a whole heck of a lot that can happen, moving forward in the right direction, until you start **behaving** in a manner consistent with your own best interests. This is true for everyone, but it's especially true if you're a person with background blemishes. Talking about it or, worse yet, complaining about it without taking positive action, is pointless.

Why is this so difficult? Why can it be so hard to leave the past in the past?

It's simple. You must now begin managing your life instead of re-living it in an ineffective way, over and over. Doing things in the same manner, time and again is fruitless. You must move on for one big reason, **the Marketplace doesn't care**. As I stated in Chapter One, understanding that the work world is changing or that you're a Free Agent is usually not very difficult to see and comprehend. But the idea that the Marketplace (the "out there" where everything happens) doesn't even care a little bit about you is a major hurdle for many.

If you are one of these people, you need to snap out of it right now. If you have even one "yeah-but" rolling around in your mind, nip it in the bud immediately. "Yeah-but" statements are mini pleas for help, re-assurance, and support. Knock it off! I'm serious. As long as you hold onto them, you're avoiding the present and not working with the tools that are really available to you.

If we were working together right now I would help, re-assure, and support your efforts. This is part of the Compassionate Tough Love (CTL) I touched on in the first chapter. However, my role would also be to represent the Marketplace as if I were a gatekeeper. As a dedicated and responsible keeper of the gate, I wouldn't think of sending you into the game unprepared and clueless to get demolished. The fact is that lingering "yeah-buts" with shallow roots simply must go. Those deeply rooted and connected to significant underlying issues must be addressed appropriately and professionally.

The straight talk is this, you are either awake or sleep when it comes to the Marketplace. Being awake means that you pull everything together and work with what you have in a smart and heads-up manner that aligns with what is in your own best interest. If you're physically and mentally capable yet mired by the past or hamstrung with anxiety about the future, there's a good possibility you're not awake and oblivious to what's real. Why? Because your thoughts and energy are focused on the past and the future—and not on the present.

In extreme cases, some people are completely disassociated with the ways of the world. These are probably not the people who will pick up and read this book. They are unable to function on almost any level, let alone compete in the no-holds-barred Marketplace of today. People significantly challenged by mental illness and active addiction broadly fit in this category.

The fact is, there are many background-challenged people hanging out somewhere in the middle. If this describes you, chances are you're not as compromised in your abilities as the people described above. Yet, you may find it difficult to sustain forward movement. If you've struggled unsuccessfully to retain a job once you've landed it, this has probably resulted in even more employment gaps and frequent start-overs. The vast range of conditions and situations impacting your employability positively or negatively, is immense. Once tossed into play in the Marketplace it all has a way of blending and blurring together.

"Employment re-entry" is a niche field that exists between the world of social work and the Marketplace. I'm an expert in this field when it comes to helping background-challenged people of every kind. Those of us working in employment re-entry are like third-leg relay runners in a track and field competition. We receive the baton on the run from the second runner in the hand-off, take our lap, and then pass it on to the fourth runner who runs the last leg of the race. The baton passed from runner to runner is you, the person who's on a journey of employment re-entry, up and through whatever system or program you're utilizing as your support.

Runner number one represents where it all begins, frequently a "bottoming out" experience like spending the night in the county jail, detox, or a stint at a regional mental health center. Runner two is the next step in the process such as prison, a treatment or rehab center, or a transitional living facility. The re-entry specialist runs the third leg of the journey finally handing the re-entering person over to the Marketplace, the fourth and final runner.

Sadly, the third runner is frequently missing. The baton is handed off from runner number two to runner number four. Unfortunately, the baton (again, that's you in this analogy) will be ill prepared and not yet able to compete. Even worse, there might not be a second runner, either. In this case the relay baton is just dropped somewhere in the middle of the track with no runner in sight to pick it up and carry it over the finish line.

Needless to say, being "dumped" back in the race, woefully unprepared, means there's a strong possibility of losing. In fact, if the baton (you) ever crosses the finish line it could end up in a wild crash and burn ending.

This is serious business. On a good day, competing in the Marketplace can be a tough go for those who are fully fit, emotionally, mentally, and/or physically. If you are burdened with background baggage, there's a high likelihood you aren't entirely prepared or fit yet. Taking on the fourth leg of the race into the Marketplace can be more than tough; it can be brutal.

But it doesn't have to be this way. There's a way to get there if you're dedicated to getting the results that will spell success, even as a background-challenged person.

The first step involves a bit of CTL and a reality check. It's time to wake up and get up. There's a good chance you'd rather not, preferring to stay asleep, tucked away in your comfort zone no matter how out of step it may be with the ways of the real world we live in now. You need a kick out of bed. Preferably, you'll do it yourself, because self-motivation is always the best way to roll. Regardless, once up it's time to smell the coffee, which means coming to the honest realization that the world does not revolve around you—with your private issues, your drama, and your "internal reality" that doesn't align with the rest of the world.

Seeing things as they really are is the whole point of the discussion about the Marketplace and the analogy about the relay race, the four runners, and the baton. Look, if you honestly can't compete due to a legitimate disability, then another route must be explored. However, you may be fully able to get out there, run the race, and compete just like the next Joe Johnson in the Marketplace. So why aren't you? You're fit, right? No sprained ankle or broken leg, yes? So why not?

It could be your thinking is far out of sync with how things really are in the world. There may be unpublished rules and guidelines concerning how the whole hiring thing operates of which you're totally unaware. Imagine a hidden manual revealing all the secrets to getting and keeping a job. Some people seem to know where to find it and others are clueless. If you have no idea how a job search for people in your situation actually works, how on earth can you know what to do? How do you proceed in a manner that is in your own best interest? Here's the right place for another favorite quote:

"When the student is ready, the teacher will appear."

I believe it is all a matter of "awakening." You may perhaps realize it in a big "ah-ha moment." Or, maybe it will come more slowly and gradually. However it happens for you, awakening is all about seeing things as they are and observing the world as it really exists. But here's an important point; the result must have neither a positive or negative charge to it. If, after awakening, your conclusion is that the world is a big f---ked up place and, once again, you've been screwed, then you're still fast asleep. On the other hand, if you blow out of bed at six o'clock in the morning, transformed and riding on a mythical cosmic light beam, take stock. You're still sound asleep and dreaming, too.

Your awakening may serve you best if it is more of a dawning. It should be neutrally charged, as if you're seeing something new for the first time. It may not seem like it at first, but gradually you'll notice an atmosphere of order and structure exists. Perhaps you've noticed more clarity and vividness around you.

Seeing the world in this way means you're able to sense your position within it without having to place a value on it. You're beginning to get it. It's starting to make sense that before you jump into any race or competition, you must first know where the game is being played and something about the rules. Suddenly it hits you like a slap to the face, "I can either wise-up and get real, or remain asleep, doomed to struggle continually in a world where the playbook is permanently hidden."

Author and speaker Steven Covey addressed this issue when describing natural social laws, similar to physical laws such as gravity and friction. Covey makes the case for universal social norms such as honesty, fairness, and integrity. I believe this is a viable concept. In fact, I've seen it manifested repeatedly working in the prison system where habitual offenders kept cycling through over and over as if they were immune to these natural social laws. It's as if, they believe somehow they're different and their version of reality trumps that of society in general. It's as if they can somehow succeed running totally against the grain and the rules of the game. They don't get it and they can't see it. Or, perhaps they do but don't know how to change, adapt, or act differently. Based on results, they're unable to align their best interest with the rules of the Marketplace which, as we know, is the environment and the landscape upon which all economic games occur.

I have one final word before moving on. You may take issue with my straight-up approach to the complexities of "people problems." I have no beef with anyone about this point. I mentioned before, one of the things I'm good at is being blunt. So, you're right, my approach is cursory, but there's a purpose in this. My education and training are based in the arena of helping others. Yet my practical experience has given me another perspective.

I believe the realities of the world we live in today cannot be ignored; this includes globalization, free agency, digitization, and the dynamic flow of the Marketplace. Encouraging you to re-enter and participate in the Marketplace if you're out of touch and not in possession of the essential tool of mindfulness, is fruitless, if not heartless. Being out of tune in this manner contributes, in the short run and long term, to cycles of incarceration, abuse, addiction, and hopelessness.

The Wrap-up

Your big task for this chapter is to identify and write down your PJO. As stated above, this may be so obvious and monumental, it hardly needs to be reiterated. If so, think again. Write it down as your first writing assignment associated with *Get Beyond Your Troubled Past*. Make it a declarative "I will" statement. "I will stay clean and sober. I will remain on my meds. I will stay away from people, places, and things that cause me trouble."

If you don't have any issues of this sort, then write down the following. "I am grateful that I don't have a major PJO, and I am willing to accept that I may have a smaller one. I commit to staying awake, alert, and ready to wrangle it to the ground the minute it shows up."

Get ready to do some planning and objective setting in the next chapter. So buckle up and roll up your sleeves, it's time to get to work.

Action Steps

Identify and write out your Personal Job One (PJO).

Practice staying in the present moment.

Chapter Three

Your Smartest Game Plan

This chapter adds two components to our job search picture, your Plan and your Job Search Objective. These elements are crucial to the overall picture and to my approach. You will encounter both of these critical elements throughout the remainder of the book. So don't skip them or treat them lightly. But first, let's meet another of our characters.

Catherine: from Timid to Success Story

Reliable and dependable to a fault, Catherine called ahead to say she was running late for our 3:00 pm appointment. No problem on my end, she was my last appointment for the day and I needed to catch up on client notes. At 3:15 pm, I heard her say, "Hi," to Jim across the hall. She knocked softly. Her head popped through the partially open door.

"Hi, John, sorry I'm late," she eased through the doorway, then hesitated. "Should I close the door?"

"Yes, please. Make yourself comfortable while I clear my desk."

"Okay, great." She closed the door carefully and sat down next to the bookcase.

Petite, thirty-seven-year-old Catherine gave the impression of still being the athletic gymnast she was as a girl. She wore her sandy brown hair cut short, fancied flats over heels, and frequently dressed in stylish sweats. Today, she came directly from work, wearing dark slacks, a gray top, and big silver hoop earrings.

Catherine's tiny stature fit hand-and-glove with her reserved nature. In fact, unless she made a concerted effort otherwise, she came across as timid, even mousy.

"So, how are things at the old glue factory?" I asked using an inside joke her current boss Roxanne once said. Catherine's cautious, methodical ways were too much for the gregarious Roxanne. "You'd think you were working in an old glue factory," she'd told us both with a big laugh over lunch. Roxanne saw the potential in Catherine immediately and went to work helping her come out of her shell.

"Just fine," Catherine replied. "In fact, Roxanne sent me to Kingman last week to train a group of new hires on the billing software we're using. That's the third training I've done. It's fun; I enjoy doing it."

"Terrific. Did you go alone?" Kingman, Arizona, is about a ninety-minute drive from Las Vegas.

"Yup. I drove over in the morning, had a mid-day session, and made it back to Vegas a little after six in the evening. Everything went smoothly, and the drive was nice."

"Wow, congrats. A big step."

I began working with Catherine while she was employed as a warehouse receiving clerk in Henderson, a suburb southeast of

Las Vegas. She aced that job immediately and even helped the company IT guy upgrade their inventory system. From there, Catherine did the same with the company bookkeeping software. Unfortunately, the company showed no interest in recognizing or rewarding her for her contributions. After doing all that and more, she remained in the tiny receiving office making barely over minimum wage.

"Thanks," she looked straight at me. "It's a big step for sure. I still feel like an imposter sometimes. Like someone will see something in me and call me out. Well, not all the time, it just shows up. It happened in Kingman during the training. I don't think anyone knew, but I did."

There's more to the story. Catherine has struggled with confidence and self-worth issues for years. The second of two abusive relationships ended with her becoming homeless. After over three years on the street, numerous arrests, and minor charges for possession and soliciting, she finally gained a foothold in a woman's shelter.

The warehouse position, which came about with help from the shelter staff, could've been a good fit. But she was shaky and tentative the entire time. She was easily intimidated and ended up being used. Priority number one was getting another job, one that would challenge and nurture her.

"You didn't let it knock you off track. You finished the training and drove home. I'm proud of you," I said, smiling at her.

"Yes," she replied, her eyes dancing.

"You pulled it off ... again. To anyone else paying attention, you were in complete control, right? All that you and Cora have been doing is showing up now. It's working."

Cora, her counselor at Community Mental Health, was and still is, the right person at the right time to help awaken and strengthen Catherine.

"Right, no doubt. I was afraid to come out of my office at the warehouse much less train anybody or travel out of town. Good stuff's happened over the last couple of years. A lot. But ...," her words trailed off. Catherine scrunched her shoulders and looked at the ceiling. "My ex showed up at work again last week."

Seriously, Though, What's the Plan?

Planning, especially life-related planning, takes focus and effort. Many people start personal planning with the best of intentions but most don't complete it. They begin with an excited, emotional burst that fades quickly once the heavy lifting begins. Or, maybe they unknowingly picked the wrong method, one raising too many difficult questions and considerations. Whatever the reason, too often no plan is the result. Time passes, life unfolds and happens, and there you are, years down the road. You've arrived somewhere but nowhere in particular. As the saying goes:

"If you haven't planned your destination, how do you know when you arrive?"

Planning and goal setting, a chore for anyone, can be incredibly demanding for a background-challenged person. It's also possibly new territory. How can this be? Setting goals and creating a plan for achieving them, requires taking action. Chances are it's more common for you to **react** which means a sudden, knee jerk response due to something else. I'll get into what it means to be proactive and reactive in the next chapter.

For now, consider background issues as the tip of an iceberg. They're big, but nothing compared to what lurks beneath the surface. "Issue-bergs" and reactive behavior tend to occur hand-in-hand; the trouble is, they won't cut it in the world of the

Marketplace. There must be a positive change yet, as we all know, changes rarely "just happen" without a concerted effort. And so it goes, the pattern of reactivity continues. Plus, maybe you have no idea even how to make plans and set goals. As a result, important things such as goal setting and life planning don't happen

Why have a plan?

I've come to believe five-year plans work best. Still, a plan is a plan and if the thought of putting one together leaves you cold or makes you uncomfortable, try using another word. How about "outline," "road map," or "blueprint for success?" Don't get hung up on a specific word or anything else about planning and goal setting at this point. If you do, there's a good possibility you'll get stuck and little or nothing will get done.

Now, read the three questions below. Think of each one in terms of becoming a goal in your mind versus a dream. Make each something big and exciting, yet realistic and attainable. In five years

- What job do you want to be working at?

- Where do you want to be doing that job?

- What kind of person do you want to be?

Avoid any natural impulse you may have to take this step lightly. Give it your full attention and consideration. You'll implement your plan to get to these goals over five years, so sleep on it if necessary, but don't drag it out. Write down the answers to all three and combine them into one statement. "In five years, I will …."

There are two primary reasons you need a Five-year Plan and Goal. First, it provides you with a route leading to your life destination or your goal. Second, the route you plot out can be used for reverse planning. Reverse planning means, you start with your destination in mind and then work backward to the present. The outcome of this planning-in-reverse is another goal, your initial Job Search Objective, covered in detail in the next chapter.

Now, go ahead and reverse it. Take a sheet of paper and draw a straight line length-ways from left to right leaving a little room at either end as a margin. Start by marking your Five-year Goal at the far right end of the line. Then go to the beginning left end and mark it "NOW." Add markers for years One, Two, Three, and Four so there is equal space between each marker. Half way between Now and One add another marker labeled "JSO (which stands for Job Search Objective).

You now have two goals, your Five-year Goal (long-term destination) and your JSO (short-term starting point). But that's not all. You also have a schedule. You're starting now and your first major mile marker is your first goal, your JSO. From there, you will encounter four annual mile markers before reaching your ultimate goal five years from now. A lot will happen in between. There will be key mile markers you'll hit along the way, which require detailed mapping, a strategy, and analysis. All that will come in time.

Why do it this way?

Your Five-year Plan and big goal provide a framework for an Objective-based Job Search which I'll delve into deeper later in the chapter. In short, this approach tackles a common problem exemplified by the following question.

Question: *"What kind of job are you looking for?"*

Answer: *"Gee, I don't know, what do you have?"*

Without a plan, you don't have a starting point. Any response similar to (a) "Gee, I don't know ...," and (b) "What do you have?" scream, "**I don't have a plan**!" Without a starting point, you become another walking example of ineffective, reactive behavior.

You're like a tiny sea creature adrift, dependent upon the ocean currents to move you from place to place. You never arrive at your destination because you don't have a particular one defined. Instead, you float along, reacting to whatever conditions turn up. For the background-challenged job seeker, this is not the approach you want to take.

If, while reading the above, you experienced "yeah-buts ..."

- *Yeah-but, what if I really don't know what I want?*

- *Yeah-but, what if I can do all kinds of different things?*

- *Yeah-but, isn't it better to keep my options open?*

- *Yeah-but, what about the economy and all the competition out there?*

- *Yeah-but, what about the alignment of the sun and the big tree in the backyard?*

If little, annoying yeah-buts keep popping into your head, knock it off. There are no real yeah-buts. In fact, they're part of the problem. People love having yeah-buts because they're like little exit doorways that prevent planning and provide excuses. If you want to succeed, don't go there.

The purpose of your plan, as described above, is to assist you in developing your personal Job Search Objective or JSO. **That's your answer** to the question above, "What kind of job are you looking for?"

Your Life Priorities List

At this point, you have your Five-year Goal, a time line, a starting point (Now), and a soon-to-be mile marker, your JSO. Good start. Let's change things up a bit. I want you to make a list of all your current life priorities that **don't include** job searching. These are real-time, "smell the coffee" considerations that must get done (things associated with family obligations, schedules, anything that should or will happen) regardless of anything else occurring in your life.

Rank the list of these priorities yourself. Now, take a break.

Before making another move, buckle up for your first lesson regarding "operating in the now." You've created your list; it belongs to you. You devised it from your perspective, laying out what you think is important, what you think needs doing, right?

Stop and take another break. I'll ask you to show the list to someone else, the person closest to you, the one with whom you have the strongest personal relationship. But listen up first. There's a high likelihood this person won't see the list the same as you do. There will be differences in what each of you thinks. That's normal and to be expected. Don't let it discourage you.

There's a real possibility your friend or loved one will bring up how things have gone in the past for you. When they do, will you

- Dig in and defend your list with this person?

- Drag in fragments of old, unresolved issues to bolster your case?

- Try to avoid something that wasn't included on your list but added by the other person?

Again, I implore you, stop!

Operating in the present moment starts this minute. Looking and discussing your list (in the present moment) requires you to refrain from dragging up crap from the past or panicking at the thought of doing something you don't want to do. It's a list. You're just working on your list. If you can't discuss the list without using it as a vehicle for traveling down the same old road again, then you're not ready.

The responsibility for getting and being ready is on you. When you can do this and stay focused on the business at hand, you're ready and able to live in the now enough to start getting your life on track. What the other person says and how they respond to your list, is out of your control. Don't react to them. Suck it up and listen. There's no room for blaming or complaining here. I've told you to show your list to this person, asking for their input, because you truly need it.

Now, thank them and walk away. Then re-write or edit your Life Priorities List, re-creating it and **incorporating** the points they brought up. Leave one line empty at the top.

Don't kid yourself, you aren't doing this as a rugged individualist, riding the range all alone. Forget what Hollywood or the advertising world would have you believe. You need feedback on how other people you respect see things, because it'll set the stage for a joint venture requiring buy-in from both of you. Furthermore, you may be the person doing the job searching, but this is not a solitary activity.

If, on the other hand, you currently live alone, recreate alone, and operate with your own money completely independent of the financial and emotional support of others, then disregard the advice above. Otherwise, take it to heart. Even if you're independent, you'll achieve your goals faster working with others. There are things that you will just have to accept (another key mindfulness concept I'll develop later in the book), and how you manage yourself regarding your own personal acceptance has a direct impact on the effectiveness of your search.

After your priority list is complete and ranked by degree of importance, put together a weekly calendar. List all obligations and commitments related to your life priorities. Include everything on your calendar. I recommend underlining items in color as a way to categorize each entry. I suggest using three colors to keep it simple for yourself. For example, underline your highest priorities in red, mid-level priorities in blue, and, your lowest priorities in black.

When your list and your calendar are complete, study it. Let it sink in. This list will remind you what is or should be happening. This isn't just from your perspective, but both your perspectives. The shared ownership of your list will have tremendous value when things get busy, schedules get hectic, and emotions become frayed.

Keep in mind the time-tested advice of "see your job search as a job." In fact, now you can add "job search" to the blank space at the top of your list. Job searching covers many different activities. For the time being, just list it as one of your top priorities that must happen every day. You won't be out meeting people, introducing yourself, and interviewing every day. But something needs to happen daily. I'll cover this in great detail in Chapters Seven and Eight.

At this point, you may be sensing the magnitude of this undertaking, perhaps even feeling a little overwhelmed.

My purpose is giving you an opportunity for a good, hard look at what you need to accomplish. Working at only life priority items on your list without including your job search won't get you to achieve your JSO. The same goes for job searching and ignoring other life priorities. You must balance both while keeping your head on straight as you progress. Add it all up and it's much more than a job. Effectively managing the priorities in your life and your job search too just became far bigger than any job you've ever held.

Your life priorities schedule

Your next step is scheduling your time. If you don't schedule it, you won't do it. Scheduling is where you decide what and when things get done. You'll discover your job search to-dos may conflict or even bump into other high level priorities on your list, making it a tough call at times. It happens. Make your scheduling choices and keep moving forward.

All these decisions are yours to make. What stays and what goes? Take a second look at your schedule, cutting and pruning items from the list. When your schedule is complete, show it to the person you've confided in. Remember, you're not alone in this process. Collaboration is essential, so make sure he or she understands what you want to accomplish. Likewise, it's up to you to incorporate their input, ask for clarification when you need it, and don't assume anything.

A thought from John

If you're not getting this collaboration stuff, especially the men reading, let me stress an important point. You may naturally think you don't need input and feedback, but you're wrong. Not only do you need feedback on your list and schedule, you should want it. There's a lot on your plate. Doing this right requires a significant amount of effort and energy. The last thing you want is a steady stream of conversations about what's not getting done. See doing this as covering your backside and a way of preventing procrastination. It's a preventive measure to manage the inevitable feelings of chaos and upset if you try to "solo" it. Trust me, ignoring this step can lead to a train wreck of major proportions.

For example, forgetting your spouse's birthday is a problem all by itself, but it can **really** disrupt your sense of equilibrium and throw a monkey wrench into your job search. A misstep of this type can knock you off track, making operating in the present, with a clear head, difficult or worse.

So do it. Show your schedule to your emotional joint venture partner, editing it as needed just as you did with your list. No whining, no attitude necessary. Just do it.

The point of this is to lay things out as they really are, not how you'd like them to be in fantasy land. Refusing to do this will inevitably lead to stress and anxiety. Eckhart Tolle, author of *The Power of Now,* defines stress as

"I'd rather be someplace else doing something else, but I'm stuck here doing this."

When it comes to both your list and schedule, the message is clear—create, confirm, own, and accept—to reduce your stress and anxiety. Get your head around the fact that what used to be true is no longer the case. Priorities may have changed but the number of hours in each day is the same. Acceptance means awakening to the fact that top priorities must come first. Everything else comes in second or is eliminated.

Staying Present

What about staying and operating in the present? Why is this so important? Because this is how things really get done. This is what it takes to make your JSO and your long-term goals happen. Using and sticking to your schedule will lead to daily action lists. Start each day with a daily list. These are things to do right now, today. It's about real time, living in the now. Take action now because that's what's on your list to do ... **now**. What happens when tomorrow rolls around? It becomes a brand new **now** and a completely new opportunity. Tomorrow you do what needs doing then, in real time.

Preparing for future events and situations is what planning is about. You plan today for tomorrow. Then put the plan away and concentrate on doing what needs doing today, right now. It's easy to ruin today because you're overly concerned, perhaps even consumed, with what'll happen tomorrow. Folks with background problems are especially prone to getting caught up this way because often there are "lots of things hanging." I understand, but it makes the need to address your situation and what's hanging even more acute.

Planning, scheduling, and implementing in the present, is a big deal. Check up on yourself numerous times each day by asking yourself:

Where am I now in relation to the present moment?

- Am I focused and operating on purpose?

- Are my thoughts wandering to the past? If so, do I feel angry?

- Are my thoughts drifting to the future? If so, do I feel stressed?

Remind yourself that none of these feelings stem from *what's happening now*. They originate either from a past, which no longer exists, or the future, which is yet to come. Either way, they exist in your mind not in the here and now. So concentrate on the work that needs to be done now. Apply yourself and accomplish your scheduled tasks in real time. Doing this will help you open a pathway to the present.

Your Job Search Objective

What are you trying to accomplish, **exactly***?"* To find out, let's make sure we're on the same page when it comes to terms. Let's define a few terms related to the type of position you want:

- **Job Search** means the process of finding employment

- **Job Search Objective** is your desired outcome at any point in the process

- **An Objective-based Job Search** is a job search strategy built around a particular objective

Putting an Objective-based Job Search into action means pursuing only those outcomes that are in alignment with your Job Search Objective or JSO. To do this, you start by defining your **Objective**. For some people this is easy, for others it's like pulling teeth. Regardless, it must be done. It's a crucial, fundamental step that will guide you forward through all phases of your search process. See your objective as your compass, guiding you forward as the clouds roll in and especially when the road ahead seems long and steep.

There's another reason for having an objective, and it's not always obvious. A properly defined objective is clear, concise, and narrowly focused. As a result, it will show you clearly **what not to pursue**. Don't overlook the value in this guidance because determining what not to do is more than half the battle. A right, tight objective provides amazing clarity concerning what to go after. It will also give you permission about what to avoid. For any pursued outcome, it's either in alignment with your objective or it's not. When it isn't, don't consider it, let it go, and move on. I must reiterate, when something is out of alignment with your goals, **let it go and move on**!

At the heart of this book is the notion that you should develop and use a highly focused objective. Taking this approach prevents you from running after job possibilities that are inappropriate. It also helps you steer clear of what I call *bonehead moves*, especially during your search for your initial position. Here are a couple of examples:

Taking a **Shotgun Approach** is blasting away, trying to hit as many targets as possible. A dedicated job search is harder than this. To maximize your odds of success, zero-in and specialize. Yes, shot-gunning may feel good, temporarily. After all, you're doing something, getting out there kicking whatever tires you can find. However, this approach scatters you, just like buckshot from a shotgun. It also places you in competition with other better-qualified candidates for the job you're taking "a shot" at. Add to this scattered approach, your background issue. Now, you tell me, who's likely to make the final cut, you or the person more experienced at a particular job?

Another completely counterproductive approach for you as a serious job searcher is the **Me-too Method**. This means the job seeker (you!) chases after leads others have found or developed. On a rare occasion, where the objectives for two people are similar, this can work. However, the odds don't favor success because it places you in a reactive mode. Remember, you're a Free Agent, which means your mission is blazing your own trail. Leave the "me too" stuff to others. Most of the strongest job leads you'll ever obtain are those you develop yourself. The time and energy you expend shot-gunning or with the me-too method are a waste. Concentrate on your own objective and avoid low return, high cost wild goose chasing.

Before moving to a more detailed discussion concerning your objective, here's an idea to consider: standing still can be beneficial. You need time to re-group and replenish yourself. Continuous movement might feel like progress but it can add up to movement just for the sake of busy-ness, with little or no purpose. Job searches require a lot of energy so bring it down and recharge on a regular basis.

Job Search Objective characteristics

As you work developing your JSO keep the characteristics below in mind. A well-considered objective will include

1. A narrow, tightly focused scope. Keep your eye on the center of your target, no shot-gunning!

2. Building on specific, detailed job duties and descriptions. Write a short job description for the position you're out to get for yourself.

3.   A possible target employer by category and type. For example, if you want to work in a restaurant, what type, family style, cafeteria, bar & grill, or fine dining?

4.   A concentration in a particular geographic location, by zip code for example. Define the area in the smallest scale possible, expanding is always easier than shrinking.

5.   Alignment with your Five-year Goal. Picture the progress line you drew between your big goal and starting point. You began with your long-term goal and worked backwards. Following the thread in reverse should lead to your JSO easily.

Determining your Job Search Objective

How do you develop your JSO? For some readers, working through the steps listed above should be all it takes. If this isn't your experience, go through the questions below to prime the pump. Imagine tossing your answers into a bucket to be mixed and re-mixed.

1.   What do you like and what are you good at? Liking what you do, plus being good at it, results in a powerful combination for success.

2.   What have you been trained to do? Employers pay attention to training, even in areas that don't directly relate to the open position. Make a list of all the training you've had over the years. Put everything in the bucket.

3.   What do you have experience doing? This is a biggie, but it's more than just your work history. Where you've worked plus what you actually did, adds up to your experience. Stretch it and think outside the box.

4.   What do others say you're good at? What you think you're good at may be different from what others see and think.

This becomes particularly true if you're firm about how you see yourself. Be brave. Ask those who know you, then listen to what they say about what you do well and put it in the bucket.

5. Is it realistic? The last thing to toss in your JSO bucket is a dose of reality. Reality looks like objectivity, not negativity. Be positive, honest, and practical.

Okay, now stir up what you've deposited in the bucket. What floats to the surface? Keep in mind, your JSO must align with the goals contained in your Five-year Plan. Pulling something out of the bucket that has no connection to your longer-term goals is pointless.

If you're still stuck, go back and review the first list of characteristics, tossing them in the mix, too. If you're still struggling, sleep on it. Your JSO should be waiting for you when you awaken the next morning.

How important is your Job Search Objective?

It's hard to overstate the value of having a clear JSO. In essence, it's your elevator pitch and global positioning coordinates rolled into one. Your JSO separates you from those only looking to pick the low-hanging fruit from those willing to work to achieve your desired outcome.

Time invested creating your objective is more effectively spent than plowing forward with no defined goals. There's a case to be made for not moving a muscle until your JSO is complete and in-hand. There's power in knowing what you want. Don't waste precious energy charging around "just to get things moving" before you're ready to state clearly and calmly what you want to achieve. As the old expression goes, "Keep your powder dry." It's good advice for maximizing the results of every contact.

The Wrap-up

I have put a lot in front of you with this chapter, but it's necessary and very important. Consider the creation of your Five-year Planning Goal and initial JSO as the two main building blocks of the process. I will refer to and provide examples of both of these ideas frequently in the chapters to come, so give this some quality time. In fact, do not continue reading until you have completed both of these tasks and your Life Priorities List too. There's a lot of ground to cover before you actually start searching for work, with a considerable investment of time and sweat equity on your part. So don't diddle around. Put your Plan, Priorities List, and JSO on paper now!

Action Steps

State your Five-year Planning Goal:

- What job?

- What location?

- What kind of person will you be?

Create your Life Priorities List.

Develop your Daily Action List.

Determine your initial Job Search Objective (JSO).

Chapter Four

Early Action Required

The first three chapters of "*Get Beyond Your Troubled Past*" laid the groundwork from which a new frame of mind can take root and grow. In this chapter, I'll explain why being proactive is the way to fly and why cleaning out the basement of old hanging issues is a must. But first, we'll meet Walter, our final character with his own unique story and situation.

Walter: Re-constructing a New Life

Walter wore the exact same clothes as everyone else yet, for some reason, he stood out in the crowd of newly transferred inmates. He was older than most, 56 years old as I later discovered. Second, he had a calm, reserved demeanor and seemed composed despite the continual show happening around him. This, plus his sandy gray hair, a small salt and pepper mustache and his slender, fit build, sent out classic banker vibes. Now that I think of it, perhaps a maître d' at an upscale restaurant. The word "distinguished" comes to mind, but not quite.

Walter had been locked up for a good while and was finally at the re-entry facility where he'd soon begin searching for a work-release job in Las Vegas. He was convicted of fraud related to an investment scheme of massive proportions. I asked him about it at our first meeting.

"John, I'm not here by mistake. I'm guilty, but a big part of my problem was my partner bailing out on me. I took the entire hit. I lost everything, literally everything. But that's done and past, I need to rebuild from here." Walter's delivery was friendly and a little more animated than his first impression suggested.

"You've been in a while ...," I said, glancing up from the file on my desk. Walter pursed his lips and nodded without reply. I continued. "From what I can see, you get on well with everyone." This was true, he moved effortlessly and easily among the inmates in his unit.

"You're right, on both accounts I guess. I don't want any trouble and yes, I've been down for a minute." I was about to interject but Walter keep talking. "Actually I've gotten to know a lot of guys in here by assisting them with letters, documents, legal correspondence, that sort of thing. It's a big help to them, and it gives me something to do. I'll be just as busy with it down here as I was at High Desert. I needed to stay occupied and get along, so I guess helping out fits the bill."

"What's your plan for job searching?" I always pose this open-ended, general question on purpose. I wanted to know what Walter had in mind considering he'd had a great deal of time to think about it.

"Sales, but I'm not sure where or what category of business. Nothing like I did before, that's out-of-bounds for me. Probably something with direct customer contact, possibly retail sales to start. We'll see; I have to get my bearings first." Walter wasn't champing at the bit like many of the other inmates to find something immediately. All fine by me. I could see he wasn't needy and impulsive, unlike those who sucked up a disproportionately high amount of staff time. Here's how he did it.

During his first couple of weeks in the work-release program, he shopped thrift stores for clothes and familiarized himself with the bus routes around the city. Then, he started going in and introducing himself at various retail businesses to develop a foothold. He went about his search in an independent, methodical manner, meticulously following the many rules and restrictions governing his life and his movements. An opportunity developed in a sporting goods store and Walter worked it hard. The manager strung him along and then changed his mind. This irritated Walter and resulted in a change of focus for him. He decided to stay close to the facility, relieved in a sense he didn't get the job because it would have taken a long time to get there by bus.

On one of his trips he visited the Planet Hollywood Miracle Mile Mall, a virtual candy store of retail possibilities. What caught Walter's eye were the art galleries. He found his target and went about painting by the numbers to nail down a sales position. His approach, beginning with introducing himself, was the same one I'll describe in this book for getting your first job. Each move he made was calculated and he frequently checked in with me for strategy sessions.

Walter absorbed it all, every detail and nuance, including the personality, behavior, and dress of each decision maker with whom he connected. He used what he learned at one gallery to position himself with another. It all paid off when one of the Miracle Mile art galleries hired him as a sales associate.

Walter went about his tasks like a cheetah stalking its prey. He seemed to never to be rushed yet he always locked in on his objective. In total it took him just about three months to secure the job which he clearly enjoyed right from the start.

Making Your First Move

In previous chapters I referenced the idea of "being proactive" several times. It's a common term many people use all the time. But what does it really mean?

Proactivity, like Free Agency and the Marketplace, is a concept found at the core of my approach to employment re-entry. It's a big deal and I want to make sure you understand exactly what I'm referring to when I say, "*acting in a proactive manner.*" I'll share a little word definition I hope you'll find interesting. Stick with me even if the thought of opening a dictionary makes you feel a little squeamish.

There are two parts to the term proactive, "pro" and "active." In this case pro is a prefix. It means forward, as in **pro**ceed or **pro**ject. In short, proactivity means **forward action**.

By comparison, "reactivity," is the opposite of proactivity. Reactive also has two parts "re" and "action." The "re" is a prefix, which means again, anew, or once more. Examples of this are **re**open or **re**generate. So, reactivity means "to take action again." The key word is **again,** which indicates that whatever the action is, it's been done before and it's being done once again.

We can contrast the two by making them into verb phases. This helps clarify the difference between them even more. Proactive means **taking forward action** (new action) verses reactive which means **taking past action ... again.** It might be easier just to say "old action recycled."

Okay, so why this detailed description of two words? Why make such a big deal over it? Think about it for a minute. Which of these two words, proactive or reactive, aligns best with creating and using a new life and job search plan? Which sets the stage for being a successful Free Agent? Which way of acting will work best navigating the mean old Marketplace? Remember, the

Marketplace doesn't care if you come out ahead or fall to the sidelines.

The answer is proactive over reactive every time. Okay, you may be thinking, I get it, but I still don't quite understand why it's such a big deal? Here's why. Because so many background-challenged job seekers I've met and worked with over the years have **major problems** in this area. Their modus operandi, or MO, is to react. Regardless of how and why being reactive developed inside you in the past, the fact remains, it's not a way of behaving that's rewarded in the Marketplace.

Unfortunately, reactive-based behavior patterns are hard to break and they're easily **re**inforced. Whoops! There's another "re" word. See, there are lots of them. For example, confrontations with the legal and criminal justice systems are case studies in reactivity. Those in authority call the shots and those affected had better **re**act accordingly. The same goes for issues of addiction and mental health interventions and treatment. You must turn matters over to others to get beyond the immediate crisis. Doing this is necessary but the entire process requires a degree of reactive behavior to work effectively.

At some point, the drama diminishes and the crisis passes. Gradually and inevitably, you're on your own with fewer and fewer "helpers" available to assist and guide your transition back to self-sufficiency and independence. The uncaring, unfeeling Marketplace looms over the hill. Now what?

You may know, down deep, being and remaining reactive won't help you implement a successful job search. But how do you go about changing from a reactive person to a proactive one?

Roger lived his adult life dependent on alcohol, a dependency comparable to "reaction-ism on steroids." He's able to take forward action now, but only in short bursts. In this way, he's like the little seagull on the beach running out for a tiny clam half-buried in the sand before the next wave rolls in. Moving ahead in a sustained way will require assuming command of his own ship and remaining there over the long haul.

Michael's been reacting to things his entire life too. In early adulthood, he found himself missing entire pages to his own personal operating manual. Ill-equipped to manage his own life, Michael must unlearn his natural tendency to act in dependent, reactive ways. He's making forward progress, but can he sustain it?

Catherine, while outwardly the most tentative and reactive of the four, will need to dig deeper to find the courage necessary to continue her journey. Can she do it? Can she avoid slipping back into reactive behavior, taking the path of least resistance instead of a path characterized by confidence and self-direction?

What each has working in their favor is a plan, a framework in which to be proactive going forward. To say Roger, Michael, and Catherine "should just be more proactive" without the foundation and guidance that comes with having a plan, is inviting them to fail. Their plan is their personal road map. Each must own it and buy into it completely. Without it, they will all soon be looking for another person (an authority) to tell them what to do.

And what about Walter? Well, he's different from the other three. His natural operating mode is proactivity, in a deliberate and measured way. He's made a conscious choice to be reactive because that's the logical way to go, given his situation. Perhaps the question for Walter is reversed, will he continue to be reactive which may serve as a break to the calculated proactive behavior that resulted in going to prison? In any case, he too needs a plan.

The down-n-dirty is this: with your plan in place, there's no more waiting around for something to happen or for someone else to do things for you. It's up to you to keep the ball in motion. Hesitation and waiting must be replaced by taking action and making adjustments to remain on course. In most cases, deliberate and thoughtful action is the best course of action.

General Norman H. Schwarzkopf reportedly said:

"Doing a hundred things quickly and adjusting to what's working, is much better than taking a long time to do a few things just right."

This is good advice. Read it as applying directly to you and your circumstances.

The moral of the story is: don't wait for something else to happen or for someone else to tell you what to do. Replace old re-action with new forward action. See you for what and who you are—a Free Agent, working your plan, on your own in the Marketplace.

Old Business Before New

Before any job search begins, cleaning up old business is a must. I'm referring to all the **other problems** lurking just offstage, unresolved issues such as

- the legal system

- credit card debt

- back taxes owed

- child support in arrears

- student loan debt

These are the old issues that have been left hanging or totally swept under the rug. The time is now to finally pull them out of the basement and lay them out on the back lawn in the bright light of day.

Dealing with old business requires **Early Action**. By early, I mean getting down to it as soon as you finish reading this section of the book. Consider this an excellent way to put proactivity to work. It also sets the stage for what's to come as you finalize and put your plan in motion. Action means doing. Just thinking about it doesn't count.

Dealing with old business is hard for many people. After all, this stuff has been left hanging and unresolved for a reason, maybe for a lot of reasons. Regardless, you simply have to get on with the clean-up because not doing it insures you'll remain in reactive mode, jumping from one touchy spot to another. You may want to move forward but these issues can and will keep coming around, pulling you back. Avoid all the drama and start the clean-up process before your job search begins.

Plus, unresolved issues have a nasty way of showing up at the most inopportune times. There's a sort of karmic connection that comes into play. If you're avoiding, procrastinating, or just plain lazy about addressing these nagging oldies, they will almost always seek you out for punishment, rearing their ugly heads, again. They will require you to **react** right when you can least afford the time and energy to deal with them.

Here's how to do it

It starts by giving up your internal struggle over what to do about your unresolved issues. You must finally take them on and resolve them. This all happens in your mind and between your ears before lifting a finger to do any actual work. In my experience working with background-challenged clients and attendees at my workshops and mini boot camps, rare is the background-challenged person with nothing stashed away in the basement of his or her past.

So join the many before you who've made the decision to tackle their oldies. There's an unexpected bonus to stepping up.

Addressing these **other problems** can often be the action that propels you to success in the early phases of your job search. The act of finally getting on with it will remove a huge, ugly, hidden barrier. Suddenly some of the blockage that's held you back is gone. The path forward is a little easier to comprehend and navigate. The decision and the act of at last stepping up becomes a powerful catalyst.

The next step is to make a list of every hanging issue. No quickie job here. Take your time and write out your complete list. Doing so can bring old memories and emotions up to the surface again. If you feel shaky, nauseous, or on the verge of a panic attack (seriously, it happens) set things aside for a few hours or overnight, but come back to it. **Do not** let these feelings discourage you from finishing the task.

If you honestly need to set the list aside for a bit, remind yourself that you already made the decision to do it and, furthermore, there are a few items already on your list. Return to your list and finish it. Do your best to remain in the present moment which will help deflect any unpleasantness from the past and uncertainly or worry over your future.

Once you have your list, the digging and piling begins. Gather together whatever files, old documents, and notes you have on hand or you can easily obtain. Cast as big a net as necessary to bring together anything and everything pertaining to all you've listed. More than likely, you'll have lots of material for one issue and little or no material for another one. That's fine and to be expected.

When you're done accumulating, separate the documents by subject. Build yourself

- A pile for taxes owed

- One for child support

- Outstanding warrants of ANY kind

- Debt in collection, student loan debt, etc.

The next step requires a small monetary investment. What you have should fit in a portable file box, the plastic type with a carrying handle that holds hanging files. You can purchase these at any office supply store. Make sure to get yourself a sturdy one. Additionally, you'll need a box of hanging file folders and a box of one-third-tab manila folders. That should do. If you need more space, get another carrying file box and whatever additional hanging files and folders you'll need.

Prepare hanging file labels for each item on your list. If there's a big pile for any one item, sub-divide them using the manila folders and/or make more than one hanging file. Put the labels on your hanging files and load in your documents.

Avoid the temptation to dump material in a big fat miscellaneous file. In fact, **don't have a miscellaneous file**! If you're unsure where something goes, create a new item on your list and new files for your box, until every document is filed in a home of its own.

Don't get cheap or lazy when it comes to this file box and folders step. As I write this, visions of shoeboxes, jammed backpacks, and dog-eared manila document envelopes come to mind— nothing but jumbled messes. If this is you, get on top of your box, files, and labels right now. Each oldie on your list should have its own file and its own folders, no exceptions here. You may be doing clean-up steps on this material for quite a while, and you'll thank yourself a hundred times over for the work you did getting everything organized.

Before doing anything else, review the list and your files in the box. Is there one item that stands out above all the rest? Is there a Big Daddy old issue requiring your immediate attention? If so, it's now your number one priority. Get on it immediately.

If you don't have a Big Daddy problem, thank your lucky stars and do the following. Select two files to work on: one that looks tough and one that looks like an easy fix. Focus on **these two** and work on them simultaneously. If you were right in your assessment, the easy one will be cleared in short order. The biggie will require further work.

Expect the tougher ones to be completed in steps, over time. Accept this. Give yourself a pat on the back for the one you fixed. Give yourself an "attaboy" or an "attagirl" for taking on the toughie. But keep it to a simple pat or two, no big celebration yet. No gloom and doom, either. You're finally organized and well on your way to clearing out everything on your list.

Now pick another two, using the same approach, repeating the steps above. Soon you'll have two small oldies out of the way and two big ones "in-process." If you lucked out, the second big one turned out to be a surprisingly easy fix. Now, you have three little ones out of the way and the first big one still in-process.

Work your way through your list until all are either solved or in-process. Don't drop the ball on this step. Stick with your clean-up plan and work at it consistently. Over time, you'll see the biggies cleared from your list, just like the little ones.

However, not all the items have to be, or even can be cleared up by the time job searching begins. There will no doubt be a biggie or two that simply can't be corrected without going through many steps. Expect this possibility. Oldies such as these take time to resolve. What's most important is sticking with the process until every last item is cleared away.

A job search benefit

There's a benefit to cleaning up old business that connects directly to your job search. Once an employer comes to know "your situation," and they will, they probably won't be surprised by the existence of oldies hanging out there. The fact that unresolved issues and big background problems usually co-exist is one reason why many employers avoid people with background challenges working for them in the first place. Lingering issues can distract and disrupt employees and be cause for unnecessary drama in the workplace.

But you've cleared up numerous old issues and are working on clearing up the rest. You have documentation proving this in your files. This material can be usable in your job search and will tell others a great deal about your level of seriousness and dedication. Consider it another arrow in your quiver. It's there to be used if and when a situation occurs where it's needed.

Outstanding warrants

Outstanding warrants, typically bench warrants issued by a judge for failing to appear in court, can be just as critical as Big Daddy issues, yet harder to spot. They can almost act like land mines, hidden and highly destructive. I use the word "hidden" with some reservation because when an outstanding warrant or the possibility of a warrant "pops-up" in the course of cleaning up all the old stuff, the three most common reactions are:

- *"Gee, I didn't know about it."*

- *"Really? I thought it was taken care of."*

- *"Okay, I knew it was there, but I let it go."*

Regardless of your reaction, the same proactive steps are needed. Deal with it immediately. If it involves a serious issue, an arrest warrant for example, consider obtaining legal counsel before going forward. In fact, sitting down with a private attorney or one from a legal aid organization is always an option for advice you may need on any aspect of the legal parts of your clean-up process. My intention is not to provide legal advice; I'm not an attorney. Instead, it's to provide insight into the usual process of clearing away outstanding warrants related to minor offenses.

Some people decide to forge ahead on their own without legal representation. This happens frequently when a person believes the warrant is minor, has little or no money to hire an attorney, or can't wait if the line for legal aid assistance is long.

Start first by contacting the judicial entity where the warrant originated. For example, contact the city or county where the offense took place. Call ahead by phone if possible before going in so you know what to expect. It may involve posting bail or spending a few days in detention until you can appear in front of a judge. If you walk into a local police department to inquire about your warrant or get your background report, you run the risk of being arrested on the spot. That's why it is best to contact the judicial district that initiated the warrant by phone first.

The point of this information is to get these ticking time bombs out of the way before they create a major disruption in your life. Imagine, finally getting the job you want and having to call your new boss from the county detention center to explain why you won't be in for a few days because you were picked up jaywalking. Well, you hope it's only a few days. This is a common occurrence. I've seen it play out in many ways, including inmates who were picked up while on work release making a call back to prison to say they were in County Detention. In other words, they were in jail **while** they were still in prison! Deal with these situations now before there's an employer in the picture.

Bad credit issues

Hanging issues that aren't criminal in nature can nevertheless impact your employment status negatively. Take a poor credit score, for example. Generally, it won't prevent you from being hired, but it can limit the type of job you're able to get. Jobs where you could be handling money will likely be out of bounds. However, having bad credit won't come as a surprise to a potential employer given your even bigger background snags, a felony on your record, for example.

Here's where being organized about clearing up old business can come in handy. If appropriate and necessary, you can show them what you've done and what you're currently working on to complete and clean up your oldies. If they are interested in you, your efforts to address and correct your credit problems (and other unresolved issues) will count in your favor.

The situation described above (showing a prospective employer what you've done to clear away old business) is an actual technique I teach and help challenged seekers use to great benefit. Cleaning away old issues is hard work. Nevertheless, keep in mind that the strategies, techniques, and recommendations I share in *Get Beyond Your Troubled Past* are based on my **actual** experiences. Others have done the field testing. If they could speak to you from the pages of this book, they'd tell you to take advantage of everything you can—and to pass it on to the next challenged person in need.

Fixing oldies takes effort and diligence, because not only is it just "plain old work" that takes doing, but also because it can drag you right back into your old nightmares. As you work at fixing them, try hard to stay in the present moment. Remind yourself you're working in the here-and-now to clear away past things so your future will be unencumbered.

So get moving; there's not a minute to lose. You'll have lots of new things on your plate very soon with little or no time for messing around with old issues. Here's what you can expect going forward as you work to achieve your Five-year Goal. You will:

- Be very busy

- Need forward-directed motion and not a backward directed focus

- Resent yourself for not addressing old issues when you had the chance

- Possibly never regain momentum from not cleaning up a thorny, old issue

Treat this part of the process with great respect. It's an area background-challenged folks frequently skip over or will dabble at correcting. I can guarantee you, old issues won't magically go away. They can make a train wreck of your job search plan and your new life. And why is this? The reason is they originated in the "The System," my next topic and something probably familiar to you.

Dealing with "The System"

This part of Chapter Four focuses on a point with special significance for our friend, Michael. Certainly, the Michael you met in Chapter Two is doing far better at managing his emotions of anger and resentment, compared to the Michael I first met. Back then, he took every organizational encounter as an assault. To Michael, **they** were disrespectful, **they** were making it hard for him, **they** wanted him to fail, and more. Of course, he wasn't completely off the mark; rudeness, unfairness, and inconsiderate behavior are easy to find. What's more, plenty of organizational staffers with their own unresolved issues act inappropriately, if not abusively, toward the people they're charged with serving.

Back in Chapter One, do you remember the discussion about the Marketplace? The system Michael railed against is part of the Marketplace, although at first glance it may not seem like it. This is because The System is massive and sovereign enough to have its own rules. However, unlike the Marketplace, which has no skin in the game, The System is different. It will act more like a competitor playing against you. Finally, The System wants to win.

The System is the sum total of all the governmental and social agencies tasked with enforcing the law, dispensing justice, and disbursing services to people in trouble and need. My definition is overly simplified because, for our purposes, that's all it needs to be. The System is what Roger, Michael, Catherine, Walter and everyone else with background issues has encountered, reacted to, and dealt with—before and during the process of turning the corner. In a sense, it's their big challenger, the competitor who actually takes the field against them.

The System is required to take on any and all opponents. Given this, you might expect a strong, formidable foe and not the lazy challenger that's most often the case. Nonetheless, The System usually wins because most of its challengers have little or no chance of victory. As a result, The System expects to win most matches by forfeit, due to an endless stream of angry, frustrated, disorganized combatants essentially handing over the fight before it even begins. Basically, this is where Michael was earlier.

There are many reasons for these easy victories. For example

- Opponents fail to show up for the match

- They try to participate with no game plan

- They toss in the towel after the first blow is struck

- They disqualify themselves by not following the rules

All these are easy wins. Consequently, The System has grown fat, lazy, and unresponsive.

Here's what I told Michael when he showed up with a bad attitude and a massive chip on his shoulder (more like a boulder) during our second session:

"For starters Michael, stop the anger and negative attitude. Our relationship is based in the present. We'll be working toward the achievement of your future goals. I understand you have a past, and I empathize to a point. Your past counts but not when it hinders the present. Second, take a few minutes to think about

what you want to achieve considering the Five-year Plan discussed in our first meeting. Next, weigh the value of your anger and frustration, what you're getting out of carrying on against The System, versus what you really want to accomplish.

"Now make a choice, right here, right now. Will you become a worthy competitor capable of stretching The System's 'game' out to better align with your goals? Or, will you remain another angry, frustrated soul trying desperately to win while you keep blaming 'them'?"

I stacked the deck with my description of The System in that meeting. In doing so, I told Michael I was trying to give him a description of how things operated within The System from the vantage point of the unbiased Marketplace. I shared with him how participant after participant, loaded with bad attitudes and carrying chips on their shoulders took to the field and failed repeatedly, like him. The most they could possibly expect was scoring points at the margin, never a clear and decisive win. If there ever was a Marketplace Report summarizing this situation, it could be summed up in one word, **pitiful**.

I told Michael winning against The System isn't the goal. What counts is taking responsibility for how you play the game. I reminded him it's always his decision to become a worthy competitor, or another angry, irritated loser of the game. This message flowed easily from me. I am well-practiced and Michael is one of many clients who've heard the message. Some get it and some don't. Some want to tackle the messenger. Regardless, I'm only conveying what I see and believe is true about The System, a subset of the Marketplace.

Michael said he got it, that he wanted to be a serious player. Although his scar tissue runs deep, he's now better at taking the field with a clear head. Michael hasn't won every skirmish but he's held his own every time since that conversation.

The real lessons Michael learned didn't come from me, they came from his experience on the field. Perhaps the two biggest takeaways for Michael are

- Lesson One - The System isn't the real foe. It's more like a murky, deep formidable swamp that must be foraged through to take the real field of battle.

- Lesson Two - The most critical encounter with The System isn't on the field, but within the mind. It's a choice: be self-directed and a heads-up player, or a near-guaranteed loser.

The Wrap-up

In Chapter Four, I introduced the "frame of mind" discussion. I will expand on it in Chapter Five. What Michael learned is applicable to all background-challenged competitors. The toughest battles take place inside you, not on the field of play in the Marketplace.

Don't skip the clean-up (perhaps one of those internal battles you're waging). There is no better time than now, before your search gets underway, to do it.

I want you to be successful. The more successful you are in accomplishing tasks, objectives, and goals, the more difficult it becomes to deal with old hanging issues **later**.

I will flatly guarantee you this: **the pain level associated with putting off oldies increases in direct proportion to the distance you travel and the number of mile markers you hit**.

Action Steps

Construct and implement your system to take care of old business.

If necessary, reflect on and recalibrate your attitude concerning The System.

Chapter Five

Your Personal Starting Point

I will plunge right into Chapter Five by stating it's a possibility that your way of looking at things may be off. It could be that the scar tissue from your past is holding you hostage or that worrying about the future is immobilizing you. In other words, it's possible you're navigating through life with a faulty map based on things that don't actually exist.

Take a moment to refer back to Chapter Two. The core message is about awakening to the importance of aligning yourself with how things are, not how you think they are. This was included early in the book for a reason.

An expression from ancient China says,

> *"How can you expect to get where you're going,*
> *if you don't know where you start?"*

It still makes sense today. You need to know where you are **right now** as you begin your journey, to have any real hope of making it to your destination. The **where you are** I refer to is neither good nor bad, it's just plain what is true. It's the place, condition, and situation where you actually find yourself at the moment. It's your all-in Personal Starting Point, your PSP.

Your PSP is your foundation. It's solid because it's actual and real. There's nowhere else from which to begin, because there's no other authentic, true point of departure. I want you to see your PSP as your platform and launch pad, rolled into one.

This chapter expands the mindset discussion introduced in the last. Let's begin with one of the vital mindset building blocks—acceptance.

Acceptance

I'll get right to the point, you'll need to accept some things. For starters, you may have to work harder than the average Joe or Jane. Plus, there may be aspects of the process that are unfair when compared to typical job seekers. Consider the need to work harder with some degree of inherent unfairness, as a fact of the game for you. The realities themselves are important but far less significant than how you manage them.

Acceptance, as I use the term and teach it to my job-searching clients, is better described as **strategic acceptance**. You have a plan in place and somewhere to begin. Your starting point is of course your PSP. As you move forward, situations and developments will pop up that don't quite fit the plan. The fact is, all plans run into obstacles. Stuff happens and plans need to be modified. Good plans account for this. Good planners know that short-term acceptance of the unanticipated allows adjustments to be made. These little course corrections don't alter the master plan; they make it stronger.

What about the people who create and implement the plans? We human beings are emotional creatures, even you, Macho Man or

Super Woman. Too often, when our boat hits a rough patch, the tendency is to jump ship, scrap the plan, and chuck the whole voyage. Rarely do we choose to accept the situation in the short run so our boat can get back on course.

The first part of the Serenity Prayer comes to mind. I use it often, although I modified the verse a bit:

"God grant me the serenity to accept the things I cannot change ... FOR NOW!"

The term "acceptance" in this context does not mean defeat. It doesn't mean being a doormat or a weenie. It means hanging in there, in adjustment mode, until there's an opportunity to resume your course and get back on the plan. Remember, your plan includes a time line. You won't be in a constant state of acceptance because you can't be in that state forever. You have mile markers to hit and a schedule to keep. You're accepting a new development, only in the short term, so you can regroup in order to get back on track.

Additionally, and this is a big one for many background-challenged seekers, don't underestimate how much energy will disappear like a puff of smoke by refusing to use strategic acceptance. This varies from person to person; however, some people literally exhaust themselves resisting. In some cases, they actually "fight" with the situation.

The primary tool to address these moments is returning to the present moment. Staying and operating in the present removes the anger fuel, originating from unresolved issues from the past. As noted earlier, very deep-seated problems may need mending through therapy and counseling. However, less intense states can be dealt with successfully by staying present.

A Word about Fairness

What's fair and what's unfair? You're better off not asking yourself this question because it's irrelevant. Your felony, substance abuse, or some other background issue, is a fact. Your plan takes this reality into account. If you're struggling with how unfair it all is, you haven't yet come to terms with it. Not coming to terms with your reality will quickly become evident to others and this will slow your progress. Your task is to go beyond the facts, which cannot be changed. Your intention should be to lessen the impact of the facts by how you handle the process.

The short-term goal of this process is finding an initial customer, then making a sale of your service to secure your initial job. Knowing you have to work harder and jump through additional hoops, is just how it is for you. The entire process laid out in this book is designed to provide you with a way of minimizing the hoops and disadvantages of your background problems. You'll probably experience unfairness, frustration, and rejection. The most effective way to lessen the impact is by sticking with your plan and operating in the present moment.

By the way, having a plan and operating in the present will place you ahead of most competitors in the Marketplace, background challenged or otherwise. Most people don't have much of a plan and don't stick to it even if they do. Few people make the conscious effort to be consistently proactive. Fewer still understand what it means to stay present. Add it up. If you dedicate yourself to working hard and stretching for your primary goal, you'll not only get there, you'll also find your journey incredibly rewarding. This may sound a bit flowery, especially if you've had the door slammed in your face a few times. Even so, stick with me. Open yourself to possibilities.

Honesty and Telling the Truth

Let's not beat around the bush here, telling the truth isn't an option; it's a requirement. Not because someone is making you tell the truth, which is being reactive and not proactive, but because this is simply how you must roll. Being truthful and honest are the bedrocks upon which integrity and trust are built. Let's face it, if you're an ex-offender or recovering addict, prospective employers will wonder if they can trust you. They'll wonder, "What's different this time?" Come on, it's only human nature.

You may be thinking, "That's exactly the point. Isn't that why I should slip and slide a little?" Don't go there.

Most likely, your employer will eventually find out whatever you want to hide at this stage. If you're deceitful or push the issue back around the corner, it'll find a way to show up unannounced at the worst possible time. Any lingering doubts or concerns about your trustworthiness will be confirmed. Seek to demonstrate, **by being truthful,** that you know there's a potential trust issue that won't disappear right away. You must be ready to state you know this, and you intend to hold up your end of the employment bargain.

If you're forthright and honest about your background information, **and** you're not hired, it's far better to know this sooner rather than later. The way you present your background issue is a matter of strategy and technique. I refer to this as "Delivering The Mail," and it is covered in detail in Chapter Eight.

Your goal should be to get this information out as soon as it makes strategic sense to do so. The last thing you want is grinding on, hoping against hope that knowledge of your problem won't come to light or, if the bad news does come out, hoping it won't make any difference. Hope is not part of your job search. Do everything you can to control your message. See this as a deliberate part of implementing your plan.

Remember, we now live in a digital age. Those wanting to know, given time and resources, will find out. Have you considered the value of not carrying the baggage around? What would it be like to remove the heavy bags with your criminal history or other background secrets weighing you down? What would it be like for you to eliminate the secrets that currently cause you to filter every interaction with people?

Seriously, if they're going to find out anyway, why not remove the ugly bag early on and under your terms? I'll teach you how to deliver **your** mail, giving you an opportunity to lighten the load and a chance to enjoy living where truth and freedom are found.

Here's an example of why being truthful counts.

Let's assume you were a little "creative" on your job application and managed to get by whatever checks are in place during the initial hiring process. You land the job. Imagine you like the job … no, let's say you **really** like it and your employer likes you too. Everything's great.

A year or so passes and you have an opportunity to move up. Great again. This new move places you in a new job category. As a human resource function of getting promoted, your file is pulled. A new, more in-depth background search is done. Guess what? There's a discrepancy found between your original application and the new search results.

What happens next? The human resources person who discovers the discrepancy passes it up the line because it's their job. The result? Well, it's not a recommendation for promotion. Instead, you're released from your employment. You're unhappy, your supervisor's unhappy. No one likes it, especially since they liked you and were in the process of promoting you. It doesn't matter. You're out the door and that's the end of the job you really liked.

But wait, it gets worse. At best, you can expect only a qualified recommendation from your immediate supervisor. You'll get exactly zip from your actual former employer. So, how to account for the year or so spent working there once you're back on the job hunt? You either lie on your application (which is bad news and needs no further discussion), or you tell the truth and face the obvious. Being stuck in a position where you must figure out how to play this, isn't a good thing. Don't put yourself there to start.

What if you're a recovering addict? Prospective employers may or may not find out your secret. Why should they find out if you remain clean, sober, and a provider of solid service?

There are actual reasons why you (a person in recovery) may want your employer to know the truth. Here's why. First, while the digital age has sent information gathering into overdrive, it's also helped foster a heightened sense of confidentiality. There's no ironclad guarantee—and you should use discretion when discussing your situation—but employers are far less likely to share information about an employee's addiction and recovery than may have been true in the past.

Keep in mind, the job at hand is not "the job" for a recovering addict. Instead, your Personal Job One (PJO), is staying in recovery. Everything else rests upon this. Your Job Search Objective is to find your customer, sell your services, and deliver the goods. So, in this way, both you and your employer have a shared interest in your continued recovery from addiction. Additionally, there's the issue of affirmation. You must carry your own water. However, having support, even if it's simply a "knowing about it" type of support, it helps. This could include bringing your sponsor to meet your boss, when and if it's appropriate.

Also, there's the "on the shop floor" situation. You may or may not work in a shop or warehouse. But the example is close enough to fit most situations. As a newbie, you'll want to fit in and be accepted. You're walking into an established work environment with a pecking order and rules, written and unwritten. Imagine newbie you, totally green and wanting very much to fit in. What if the gang heads to the local bar and grill each Friday after work for beer or margaritas? Outing's like this can be as much a part of work as the work itself. You're included, perhaps expected to go, especially because you're the new person. But you haven't delivered the goods about your situation. You tell yourself you'll tag along and just have coffee or a soda. Right. Don't let this, or any other variation on the same theme, happen. You know your recovery is in serious jeopardy.

Your PJO is staying clean and sober. Your success, probably your survival, depends on finding an opportunity to stake out your turf early in the game. Your antenna needs to be up and functioning as soon as your feet hit the floor. Ask yourself: Who's in charge? Who's calling the shots? Who's the team leader?

That's who gets your mail delivery *before* any compromising developments happen. Remember, you're there first and foremost to provide good service, not to make friends. In spite of your desire to fit in, the cost of slipping on your PJO is huge. **You want** them to know and **you want** to be the one doing the informing. Do it right and the co-worker relationships you develop will be even stronger.

Roger: Getting Back on His Feet

Work was easy to come by for Roger in the early 1990s. He started as a laborer for a general contractor, building private homes. With a strong work ethic, Roger moved up quickly, landing a spot on the drywall team. He was young, healthy, and enjoyed the workout hanging sheet-rock gave him every day. The money was good and so were the opportunities. By the mid-90s he learned painting as well, broadening his skill base and his income. Roger was seldom without work and had no difficulty providing for his wife and two small children.

In 1997, he took a job across town with a fast-growing contractor. It was a good opportunity, providing Roger with a chance to advance to a supervisory position running two busy painting crews. The workload grew quickly. Soon it was more than he could handle. Rather than discuss the situation with his boss or make a move, Roger pressed on. So did his drinking. Two years later, he was out of control. He lost his job, his marriage, and ended up in a drug and alcohol rehab center for three months.

In 2001, Roger was sober for a little over a year when he moved to Las Vegas to be closer to his sister. Work was inconsistent for the first couple of years, but things improved as the economy ramped up in tandem with a growing housing market. Roger was now working 50–60 hours a week, making great money again. He remained sober and at the top of his game. He was a happy guy. In 2006, with the housing bubble headed to its peak, Roger received the job offer of a lifetime. He was recruited by a painting contractor building high-end tract homes a few miles southwest of the Las Vegas Strip. The money was exceptionally good, and he jumped onboard.

Unfortunately for Roger, the crew leader was a partier of epic proportions. Roger started drinking again and using drugs along with most of the team. But he held on, getting busier and busier, spinning further and further out of control. Then the party stopped. The economy crashed in late 2008 and so did Roger. He ended up in detox again after nearly killing himself.

The second rehab was difficult. Physically and emotionally exhausted, Roger moved in with his sister and her husband in 2009, working small jobs where he could. The building scene in southern Nevada was on the rocks. But, fortunately, he'd somehow managed to keep most of his savings and even without much work he helped out his sister's family while he re-gained his footing.

Little by little, Roger gradually found work. After all, he was experienced and accomplished at both drywall and painting. The money was a fraction of what it was a few years earlier, but it was enough to get by. However, after a number of years of living with his sister and her family, Roger knew it was time to find his own place. This stressed him out, as did the thought of returning to painting full time. The Roger I met was anxious, uncertain, and stuck.

Your Sales-based Approach

What do you mean, I'm in sales?

By now, you understand that you're an independent Free Agent operating within the Marketplace. Realizing this is good, but what are you out to accomplish? The quick answer is you want a job. But what does this actually mean to you?

In practical terms, it means selling your services to another party. Having a job shows you've accomplished this objective. You made the sale, and you will continue selling your services on an ongoing basis, as long as you remain employed. Before this happens however, you must find a potential customer. Once found, your goal is influencing the interaction so you have an opportunity to sell your services to that customer.

The process of selling and buying takes place whether you're conscious of it or not. The fact is that most of us don't look at searching for a job from this angle, you too perhaps. You've probably never analyzed what happens when you get hired. You're relieved to have a new job and maybe you're a bit stressed about starting it. But it's probably a safe bet you didn't reflect on the entire process from a seller/buyer perspective.

Regardless of your thinking at that moment, consider your quest to find and secure employment in terms of the sales process. Place yourself in the seller-of-service role and consider the following:

- What services do you offer and hope to sell?

- Who's interested in purchasing these services?

- Where are they located?

- How best to connect with them?

These are fundamental questions I'll cover in the chapters ahead. For now, consider you're in a selling position and your future employer is in a buying position. Let the fact that your goal is to eventually make a sale (which means become employed) fully sink in.

Don't cheat yourself, though. Don't give this a quick mental, "Sure, right. Okay, fine," before moving on to whatever else pops into your head. **This is a critical concept**. Getting it can change how you search, how you handle yourself once employed, and how you progress the rest of your working life. If I could send up a flare, I'd do it. No bull, this is a game changer.

Guess what, there's a manual available. In fact, there are hundreds of manuals and countless sources of information on selling skills. Just visit your local library or bookstore. Check out the business and selling aisle or go online and type "selling" into the Amazon search box. You'll find a ton of information ready and waiting. Yet, the idea of applying this approach to finding a job or succeeding on a job once found, must be completely foreign to most people because few apply this wisdom.

Why not?

- Why don't more people see we're all in business, in one form or another?

- Why don't they see there's selling taking place?

I believe it's because most of us **expect to get instead of give** when it comes to gaining employment. If so, it's wrong-headed and counterproductive thinking. Whenever money is exchanged for something, a sale takes place. To get paid, you give or provide something. Regardless of the specifics, if you're an employee you exchange your services for a paycheck. And in doing this, you become part of the delivery system of whatever is sold by your employer. Simply said, your job is providing **the service of doing** whatever job you're assigned to do.

This is the basic business arrangement applicable in all employer-employee relationships. Nonetheless, the essence of this situation must be hard for many to grasp, considering the two reasons most wannabe sellers of services are fired, because they:

- Could not get along with others

- Could not follow company policies and procedures

By failing to provide a service acceptable to the customer, the business arrangement is severed. There will be no further sales to this particular customer. As sales skills author Stephan Schiffman says in his many books,

> "Nothing happens in business until something is sold."

It's so true. It's an ugly day when anyone loses their only customer and must find another. It's an extremely ugly day when you have to do it with background baggage.

Marketing comes first then selling

Writing this chapter, I deliberately jumped ahead a bit to drive home the point that you're in sales and the best job search approach is a sales-based approach. However, before any selling takes place, marketing must happen. I define the difference between marketing and selling as

- **Marketing** is getting them off the couch and in the front door.

- **Selling** *is getting them from the front of the store to the back and ringing them up.*

This isn't an original definition. Nevertheless, it's a handy one to use because it's simple and graphic. Before anything is sold, it must first be marketed. This means that before you purchase something, you must be aware of it. From awareness comes interest. From interest comes a desire to have it—and, thus, you get off the couch and take action. The process involves a sequence of steps. Every step must be seen in a positive light by the potential customer or the sequence stops. Obviously, if the steps come to a halt, the chances of a sale occurring plummets.

A familiar job search expression that we've all heard and perhaps used is, "You have to sell yourself." This tried-and-true, self-promotional saying has caused untold frustration and disappointment because it puts the cart way ahead of the horse. On the surface, we get it. You need to step up and present yourself, to put yourself out there positively and affirmatively. Fine. Unfortunately, many people implement this expression without a solid plan or a well-defined JSO.

How can a prospective employer buy your services if they're unaware of them? Stepping down a level, how will your potential customer

- Know what services you offer?

- See you as *the* person to supply those services?

- Perceive you in a positive way?

Drilling down even further, how do you, as the seller, exert influence during all contacts and interactions with your prospective customer? What can you do to set the stage for an eventual sale?

Famous enterprises everywhere spend enormous sums of money on marketing for one reason—it works. The need to get us off the couch is clear to them. Businesses either do it or no sales happen. They know they must create interest and influence potential customers *first*! They understand their competitors are hard at work doing the same thing. All this is crystal clear.

Businesses know they're Free Agents. They're competing in the Marketplace, and they must market their products and services. So why is it any different for you, the job seeker? You're in business just like them. You're hoping to make a sale. You operate within the Marketplace. Why is the situation any different for you than for Nike, Pepsi, or Apple?

It's not.

If you try jumping to the bottom line to sell yourself without marketing, you'll fare no better than any other business that makes this mistake. The difference is successful businesses rarely skip the marketing step. They may misfire at times, but they don't often get ahead of themselves or overlook this step. Sadly, many job seekers do skip it. Many have no idea they should even consider it.

The Wrap-up

Throughout the remaining chapters, I'll return to the basic concepts of marketing and selling, applying them to job seekers like you. The Sales-based Approach, Free Agency, the Marketplace, and an Objective-based Job Search will guide you in conducting your own successful job search. I believe these concepts apply to everyone, but especially to you.

Action Steps

Determine your Personal Starting Place or PSP.

Commit yourself to accepting what you cannot change **for now.**

Dedicate yourself to truthfulness and honesty because it's the right thing to do and very much in your best interest.

See yourself as being in business for yourself from this day forward.

Chapter Six

It's All About Communication

Chapter Six examines how you project and present yourself to others in the context of searching for employment as a person burdened with a background issue. It's not my intent to cover each of the three sections (Communication, People Skills, and Social Media) in A-Z fashion. Rather my purpose is to present them to you with two goals in mind:

- First, to give you a starting point, an introduction to each topic so you can examine it from your own perspective.

- Second, to consider each subject from the niched down viewpoint of how it applies to you and your unique situation.

The Digital Revolution has given rise to a new way of looking for work. Some authors literally call it, "The New Job Search." It's an approach utilizing the power of the Internet. This New Job Search is quickly becoming the standard for professional job seekers and almost everyone else. In an "out-of-the-box" way, it's useful to only a tiny percentage of background-challenged job searchers. Therefore, you need to know where and how communication, people skills, and social media fit in the grand scheme of your search.

Communication Skills

What you meant to say is not what counts …

Communication is a big subject. The word *communication* is literally everywhere. It's used in hundreds of different ways, supporting a myriad of purposes. It's overused, tossed about casually, and taken for granted. It's easy to get lost in this big, all-encompassing category. But don't let it overwhelm you because communication is the heart and soul of any job search. So let's break it down and re-mix it, defining the scope of what communication means to the challenged job seeker.

For the time being, let's eliminate mass communication from the discussion. I'll touch on this later under social media. Next, to make a complicated subject more manageable, we'll place the emphasis on the communication between two individuals. This is after all, what you'll actually experience as you put your plan in motion.

For our purposes, communication involves two individuals passing messages back and forth. One person is the sender; the other is the receiver. Both the sender and the receiver are people—living, breathing, human beings. As a practical matter, the only way a person can receive messages from another person is through our five senses: sight, hearing, smell, touch, and taste.

Obvious, right? Okay, stick with me. Imagine there are two women standing face to face, about three feet apart. One woman is sending messages. She's speaking to the other woman, gesturing with her hands and arms. Occasionally, she reaches out and lightly touches the other as she speaks. Also, she's wearing a pungent, heavily scented perfume. Unfortunately, the other woman doesn't respond because she has no sense of sight, hearing, smell, touch, or taste. She has no idea the other woman's even in the room. Follow along as I switch "on" the senses, one by one, in reverse order of importance to you.

First, her sense of taste is switched on. She can now pick up some of the odor of the strong perfume, but nothing else. Taste buds are activated by odors.

Second, her sense of touch is turned on and she feels the light touch of the other woman and the air circulating in the room. If she were to guess about the person nearby it would be that she's female adding together the clues of the light touch plus the scent, but nothing more.

Next, her sense of smell is activated and she suddenly smells the strong perfume. She also smells cooking odors from the kitchen down the hall and the flowering tree in full bloom just outside.

Her auditory ability is switched on next and she now hears a woman's voice. Its high pitched and coming at her rapid fire, describing a party she attended the night before. She can also hear the woman's shoes softly clicking against the floor as she speaks, the hum of the air conditioner, and other people talking nearby.

The woman receiving the communications can now say with certainty that the person communicating to her is a woman. Most likely, she's an older woman given the tone of her voice, her pattern of speaking, and her choice of fragrance. But she can't confirm these assumptions because she lacks the one sense that accounts for most of the data we receive—sight. She can't see the other woman. Is she tall with long black hair, wearing tasteful makeup, a green dress, high heels, and a wedding ring? Is she smiling? Are her arm and body gestures big and frequent? Does she move forward as she speaks? Is her skin brown and healthy?

There's a bottom line to this and a thousand other bits of information being received. Even without the ability to actually see, her mind totals it up in a nanosecond and ... **bam**! She's mentally categorized the other person. A first impression is made and is on file in the permanent records of her mind.

This impression will be confirmed or altered by what her sense of sight produces. Perhaps the visual image will be different from the one created via the senses of taste, touch, smell, and hearing. Chances are the visual image will over-write (in a big way) the previous impression, yet something of the pre-sight impression will remain. And the greater the distance between the pre-sight impression and the visual impression, the more incongruent the overall impression will be.

Throughout the book, I will refer to being in "alignment." In the context of communication, alignment means producing a congruent impression, one where the pieces fit together to form a complete picture. Using the example above, this means an impression that's the same **before and after** the sense of sight has been switched on.

In real life, first impressions are made in three to eight seconds. They're based primarily on what the receiver sees, hears, smells, and feels, in that order. Taste doesn't usually factor in. So, the first essential communication lesson you must get is this: when meeting someone for the first time, you make an impression the instant you walk through a door, perhaps from fifty feet away. Before saying a word or shaking anyone's hand, you communicate something which becomes a lasting impression.

Refer back to the old job search expression to "sell yourself." Well, the fact is, in these few seconds, you don't have an opportunity to sell anything, much less yourself. You've already been judged and evaluated from across the room and placed in one of two categories.

1. "Okay, proceed forward."

2. "Not okay, you're done."

It's as simple as that.

I've jumped ahead in the overall discussion to make a point. What counts most is not the messages you send or intend to send, it's what's received on the other end. Communication in the context of job searching needs to be targeted and purposeful. The effectiveness of your communication will be determined by one factor, **how it's received**. This isn't a radical, earth-shattering concept. Generally speaking, we get this; it makes sense. So why is it overlooked? Here's why.

When the sender focuses only on what they're sending and the receiver focuses only on what they're receiving, there's plenty of room for error. The sender thinks they've sent a particular message. The receiver goes with whatever is received. One or the other may check in to make sure, which can improve the communication. However, it's not as good as when both sender and receiver check in with each other and confirm. When the sender focuses on what the receiver actually receives, and, the receiver focuses on what the sender is actually sending, the most effective communications occur.

Okay, but in real time things happen fast. You don't have the opportunity to check in and confirm what another person is actually receiving from your communication the instant you walk through the door. But, you can **focus on what they're likely receiving.** In other words, make sure you do everything possible to project or communicate the image you want to project. Keep in mind, it's all about what the other person receives that really counts. You can't control or guarantee what they receive because your image or message must go through the other person's unique set of perceptions and filters. However, you can manage your side of the communication by looking and acting in a way that aligns closely with **how you want them to perceive you**.

The search process introduced in Chapter Five is similar to the sales process. Your goal is selling your service to a buyer, an employer. Securing a job would be much easier if you laid everything out, piece by piece, with the time you need to present yourself so there would be no other reasonable conclusion than hiring you right on the spot. Unfortunately, you can't control the other party. Regardless of how much you want a certain outcome, you can't make anything happen with certainty regarding a prospective employer. You can influence the outcome to your benefit, however. This is why it's vital to understand how communication comes into play.

Most people think first about what's being sent, rather than what's received. Consider this in terms of your Job Search Objective. Imagine if you could send your JSO as a twin message whenever you project an image, a sound, or a smell. Hence, the receiver takes in both messages simultaneously. The question is: will these tandem messages match or align, in the perception of the receiver?

For instance, say your JSO is to be a Graphic Designer. You walk into a room and the hiring manager for the ideal graphic design company you'd like to work for is sitting there. Zip, off go your twin messages, your JSO and your initial communication; perhaps your image, voice, and handshake go too. Will the two messages fit so tightly they are received as one blended, congruent message? Or, will they arrive separately and out of alignment? If the second is true, the impression received by the hiring manager for the job you want is likely to be "off" and incongruent.

Your goal should avoid any misalignment, not just in face-to-face communications but in all communications. Take email, for example. Your message will be received and taken in visually, but it's processed as if it was heard. What will the receiver "see" and "hear" in their mind as they read an email from you? Will your JSO, like an invisible twin traveler, come through and align with what you want the other to receive?

Remember, you can't force or manipulate the outcome. The task is to manage your side of the communication. Know what you want to convey and concentrate on conveying it exactly. To get it right, walk in the other person's shoes. Experience your communication as if you actually were that other person.

When it comes right down to it, none of us can actually experience the world like another person. Each of us interprets and perceives in our own way, based on our unique personality and the sum total of our life experiences. Consequently, you'll never know exactly how you're perceived. The point is to make an effort to be the receiver of your own communication before sending it. Doing this allows you to make important tweaks and adjustments in your approach. Your aim is identifying and removing anything that could cause the other person to conclude, consciously or unconsciously, that something's "off."

Envisioning how others receive what you communicate requires honesty and objectivity. It means practicing in front of a mirror and asking people close to you for feedback. You may need a written script to practice until your introduction flows effortlessly. You may also need to adjust your "look" and wardrobe. The point is that you must be willing to modify *what* and *how* you think you're communicating. So, buckle up and accept ownership and responsibility for **what's received** by the other person.

First and foremost, you need to buy into the concept that your communication needs to be tailored to support your JSO. This has to make sense to you. When it does, you'll organically take ownership of this idea. So, **own it before** it's even sent. Do this by making sure you've done everything you can to align what you're communicating with your JSO.

People Skills and Success

Success in the workplace stems from the ability to get along with other people. In fact, experts tell us this ability, typically referred to as people skills or "soft" skills, accounts for a whopping 85 percent success rate versus 15 percent attributed to technical skills and knowledge. Viewed another way, the number one reason people are fired or fail in a job is because they couldn't get along with others.

Here's the catch. Hard skills, like learning a new software program or how to drive an eighteen-wheeler, are tangible and teachable. People skills are less tangible. These are the qualities that determine your ability to manage your behavior and get along with others. Compared to technical skills, it's difficult to sit someone down and literally teach them people skills. However, improvement in your people skills can happen. You're not stuck.

Let's start by determining what the term "people skills" actually means. The resource, Businessdictonary.com, provides a solid definition:

"A set of skills enabling a person to get along with others, to communicate effectively, to resolve conflicts, and to achieve personal and business goals."

The first attribute in this definition is the ability to get along with others. This is the **universal** ability found in nearly every description of people skills, interpersonal skills, and emotional intelligence. Your job may not require a full array of communication and inter-personal skills. Yet, it's difficult to find situations where the ability to get along well with other people won't impact your overall success.

Authors and influential thought leaders like Daniel Coleman, author of *Emotional Intelligence*, Steven Covey author of *7 Habits Of Highly Effective People*, and Jim Collins who wrote *Good To*

Great, have written extensively on what creates effective, outstanding leaders. The common thread connecting their work is the ability to understand, motivate, and get along with others. Some great leaders are blessed with it from day one. Others have worked hard at improving their people skills. At the end of the day, there's a powerful link between people skills and success.

So what about you? What's in your tool bag when it comes to getting along? If you're like most people, you're good at certain "people things" and maneuvering certain "people situations," but not perfect. In the best of all circumstances, you'd make an effort to brush up on your skills in this area.

I recommend you make this a "best of circumstances" situation. Take a look at the four suggestions below. They're simple and obvious yet people plow past them all the time without a thought. Start using them now so they gradually become more comfortable for you. Continue using them as you begin your job search. There will be opportunities to practice and polish these "skills" once you start working.

Know the norms

What's normal, usual, and expected in terms of behavior, dress, and personal presentation in the work environment you're targeting? I'm referring to basic things. For example, people don't wear flip-flops in **that office**. Okay then, what kind of shoes and clothing do they wear? Answer that question and you're on your way to fitting in. Simply looking like others isn't the goal. It's not even an actual people skill. But it's an example of something most people who possess a full set of people skills know how to do.

Observe and understand

This is connected to knowing the norms. You come to know and understand in a hurry by watching and observing others. To do this, get out and actually look at what's happening in the work environment or one similar to the one you're targeting. Seeing what others do and how they act requires you to put yourself in situations where you can observe.

Mirror what you see

Once you have an idea of what's expected (you know this by what others are doing), look in the mirror, literally and figuratively, and compare what you see with what's expected. Your goal is to see, reflected back at you, the image of others who are already doing what you want to do.

This mirror isn't static; it's interactive. Use it for practice. Introduce yourself in this mirror. Do you look, move, and sound the same as other people already there? Have short, succinct, honest conversations with the mirror. Do you sound like others sound?

Change, adapt, act

If I could help you instantly transform into the perfect candidate— the one with all the great people skills needed to impress and succeed immediately—I'd do it. That would be great. But change, real behavioral change, is hard and takes time. Therefore, the next best alternative, given a short timeframe and limited resources, is to adapt.

Adapting means to take the tools you already possess, then add and modify them to better fit each situation. Perhaps you're already fairly good at conversation. However, you get nervous when it comes to walking up to someone new and introducing yourself. If so, the fix is simple, practice. Begin practicing in front of your mirror buddy and later with trusted family and friends. Do it over and over until the process of introducing yourself comes naturally. You may still be nervous but that will disappear quickly when you practice and prepare at home. By the way, **this really works**. The only way it won't work is if you don't do it. So do it.

Some people really struggle with people skills. For all practical purposes, change is almost impossible for them. Adapting is challenging, too. Either their behavioral base or their confidence level is limited. If this is you, what should you do?

The answer is to act the part—literally see yourself as an actor on stage or screen, learning a script and playing a role. This doesn't mean becoming a robot, memorizing words, and mechanically moving from point to point on set. It means pretending you're the actor, a person different from you, moving through the scene completely capable of mimicking the expected role in a relaxed, flowing manner. It doesn't mean "fake it 'til you make it" because you aren't faking. You're still you. You're simply making your best effort to connect, communicate, and interact with others to move past the critical first three to eight seconds where impressions are formed.

I recall watching over and over as young men left a local prison re-entry facility out for a day of job searching. Too many went to prison at a young age, with little or no "real world" work experience under their belts. Out they went, tattooed and holding up their oversized pants. They were about to slink-walk to a warehouse nearby, coming face to face with the office receptionist, Becky Sue. Their people skills were honed "on the yard" and their reference group was mainly other inmates. They were clueless. Becky Sue wasn't impressed, nor was the Marketplace. Without making adjustments or acting the part, they were destined to repeatedly fail until they awakened to what the Marketplace was communicating.

The takeaway message is that your success, like everyone else's, will be largely based on your ability to get along with others. This means you may have to make adjustments to appeal to the person making the hiring decision in order to be perceived as more likeable. Modeling behaviors and acting the part will help you get a foot in the door and meet new people. However, real change comes from placing yourself in situations where these new behaviors can be used and repeated consistently over time.

Catherine Gets Unstuck

The ability to communicate and get along naturally with people are not skills shared by everyone. Catherine is a good example. She has described herself as shy, preferring to read about something versus doing it, and she prefers to listen as opposed to speaking up for herself. As a child, she enjoyed the quiet of her room. She chose her dolls and toys over the rough and tumble play of her siblings. At a young age, she recalls being repulsed by arguments and conflict. This characteristic remained with her into adulthood, ironic when you take into consideration her life situation over the last two decades.

How things turned out for Catherine while working in the warehouse comes as no surprise. For starters, she didn't find the position on her own. She got it with little effort because someone at the women's shelter where she lived knew someone in the warehouse. She was easy to recommend as she was intelligent, well mannered, and more than capable around computers. Plus, Catherine was neat and well organized, a perfect candidate for a detail oriented, shipping and receiving office job.

Catherine reacted to the opportunity as she always did. She went where she was told to go and spoke only with the person she was told to speak to about work matters. She was polite and agreeable, asking few questions. The supervisor conducting her interview liked her and forwarded her application along to the HR department with a recommendation she be hired. With no felonies on her record, her background problems didn't prevent her from employment. However, they did raise a few concerns. Catherine was asked to return for a second interview with the warehouse manager. The second interview also went well, and she was offered the job subject to passing a drug test. She passed easily.

So far, so good, or so it would appear, but not really. Her supervisor, a dock foreman named Victor, was self-centered, chauvinistic, and concerned only with how things played out for him. During one of our early sessions, I asked Catherine about Victor.

"Oh, I didn't meet him until after I was hired. There was an orientation for new employees in the morning. After lunch I was told to go to the shipping and receiving dock and report to him, and I did."

"What was your impression?" I asked her.

"I knew immediately there would be problems. Just one look and I knew. But I wanted to work there so I went with it. I felt I had no choice."

Catherine was the picture of reactionary thinking, dependency, and subservience. People like Victor are perpetually on the lookout for individuals like Catherine because controlling and manipulating others is their mission in life. She fell right into his grip, and he didn't miss a beat intimidating her. When it came to the job environment, Catherine not only failed to communicate what she wanted, more importantly she never discussed what she didn't want. In fact, she didn't communicate much of anything. She just went with the flow. Getting along by being reactive and subservient, doesn't win the game when it comes to people skills. It's not about getting along "at all costs." It's about using a degree of social intelligence. This was stifled and hidden inside Catherine.

And Victor? Unfortunately, there are Victors everywhere waiting in the wings for an opportunity to play out their twisted games of manipulation and abuse. They're adept though devious in communicating on their terms. They use the people skills they possess in unhealthy, deceptive ways. People with background challenges can be easy prey for the Victors and Victorias of the world, especially when they don't see themselves as being a heads-up, pro-active, Free Agent.

Regardless of how you see yourself, if you have a background snag, you play the game at a disadvantage. You know this and probably struggle when you're confronted by a Victor type, too. People like Catherine will succumb but others struggle differently by lashing out, for example. Of course, this can backfire, merely fulfilling the perception that they are "a troubled individual" with a background issue.

Leaving the warehouse job was imperative for Catherine. Once again, she found herself stuck in an abusive cycle. She needed to re-group and start fresh. As long as she remained cemented to her role as a reactive follower, there was little hope of reaching her personal wheelhouse and taking control of her own ship. Catherine needed to get out and break the cycle.

Social Media: Less Is More

Let's all start on the same page. I like this two-part definition of social media by Investopedia.

Part One:

> Internet-based software and interfaces which allow people to interact with each other, exchange details about their lives such as biographical data, professional information, photos, and up-to-the-minute thoughts.

Part Two:

> Social media originated as strictly a personal tool used to interact with friends and family. It was later adopted by businesses who wanted to take advantage of a popular, new communication method to reach customers and

buyers—by informing them of sales and offering special coupons, for example.

Social media is part of the "all things digital" phenomenon swallowing our lives. It started as one thing and has morphed into a many-headed thing. Honestly, it's all still very new. Individuals and organizations alike are dealing with and adjusting to the implications of social media.

When it comes to you and your background challenges, think of social media in terms of **less is more**—in fact, less to the point of almost nothing. There needs to be specific, compelling reasons for you to have a social media presence. If you can't come up with good reasons, think beyond less is more and figure zero is best. Stated another way, the greater your background problem the smaller your digital footprint should be.

Why is this so?

Look at the definition above again. What started as a **personal tool** is now an **"everything tool."** Social media is everywhere. It's used by nearly everyone, and it continues to grow exponentially. It's part of the paradigm shift and Digital Revolution discussed in Chapter One. Information about you isn't limited to official records and documents; it can be found in many places on the web because of something you or someone else posted or uploaded about you.

Chances are good none of this information has much to do with your new employment search or your plan for the future. Also, it might be unfavorable, inaccurate, or incomplete. So, approach this area like the big boys in business. They aim to own and control their message and so should you. Why be any less determined and single minded than they are when managing information about yourself? You shouldn't be and here's what you can do about it.

Social media search

Start by making a list (I know, another list!) of every internet site with information about you. This includes websites, online memberships, email accounts, chat groups ... anything where you have a presence, no matter how small and ask yourself

- Where have you had a web presence of any sort?

- Where have you posted comments?

- Where have you shared or uploaded pictures or videos?

Make your list from memory first. Next, Google search yourself using all variations of your name. Do the same for any aliases or nicknames you've used. Consider using other search engines too, comparing their results to what you discover on Google. Record everything you find on your list.

Take a good look at what your list includes. Ask yourself the following two questions in relation to every item listed and everything you've discovered about you, online:

- What does this have to do with my **new** Five-year Plan and my **new** JSO?

- Placing yourself in the shoes of an owner or hiring manager, ask, "If I were hiring, would this information influence my decision to hire or not hire **me**?

Notice that I didn't give you a neutral choice such as *this information would have no impact on your JSO either way*. I asked the question like this on purpose because, when it comes to getting your foot in the door and achieving your JSO, there's no neutral choice. Information about you either helps to increase your chances of being hired, or, it hurts you and decreases those chances. It's that simple. There will be plenty of opportunities to rebuild your internet presence later, if necessary. For now, you want to keep things bonehead simple. If it helps, it **might** stay; if it hurts in any way, it **goes**.

Now comes the real work. Start with the biggest potential problems. If you're not sure which are the biggest, start with the ones easiest to find when conducting a Google search on yourself. Go to each site and do what you can to remove the information. This can mean logging in and deleting, closing accounts, or pulling down websites. Expect this to be a project like cleaning up old business as we discussed in Chapter Four. Use what you learned to stay organized while cleaning up The Digital You on the web. Some things clean up easier than others. There's no doubt you'll have to make a few phone calls and send a few emails. You may even have to send a few snail mail letters. Do what it takes.

A social media search will probably lead you to websites that accumulate and sell publicly available personal information including addresses, phone numbers, and court and criminal records—all sorts of public record data. Many of these websites have an "opt-out" method where you can request your information be removed. However, there's a big difference between social media-related information and publicly available official documents. If you have two felonies that haven't been expunged or sealed, don't expect the "opt out" route to take care of your problem.

Even if you're successful at removing the information distributed by a particular site, the official records such as your driving record, felonies, misdemeanors, marriages, lawsuits, etc., will remain unchanged. Nonetheless, you may benefit by finding inaccuracies via your internet search. If this happens, don't panic. You just discovered something you didn't know yesterday. The fact that **you found** this information is what's valuable to you at this point. There are ways to correct inaccurate public records, and I'll expand on these in Chapter Seven.

A word to professional or traditional "white collar workers" who are challenged job seekers—you may still have an extensive Internet presence on LinkedIn, professional organization sites, recruiter sites, company sites, your own website(s), and more. Review the two questions above for yourself. Even though all your professional information may be presented in top-notch fashion, ask yourself

- Does it apply to me now?

- Am I returning to the same line of work?

- Will existing social media information help or hurt me?

Were you a dental technician, registered nurse, or physician with a felony conviction who lost your license due to drug use? If so, you won't be returning to the same line of work in the near term, if ever.

Were you a real estate professional convicted of fraud? Or a financial professional convicted of embezzlement? In these and other similar situations, you will be unable to obtain a license in your former industry, perhaps for life.

I can put faces to former professionals re-entering the workforce in a capacity different from their previous career field. Many professionals find it hard to dis-identify with their former selves. For these people, removing their social media presence can be almost like erasing themselves. Is this you? Do you want to hold onto what you used to do? Does part of you want to show others what and who you used to be?

Remember, there's sure to be a computer keyboard inches away from anyone considering you as an employee. Regardless of what is allowed or not allowed in terms of formal record checks, tapping your name into a search box takes only a few seconds. You will be **whatever that person discovers about you** on the Internet. Make sure there's no misalignment. Don't pile additional problems on top of the background issue that compelled you to seek help from this book.

If the above applies to you, take time to copy all your social media information to a thumb drive or print it out. Tuck it away for later use, if needed. Then, get on with eliminating your former professional self from any and all social media and Internet sites. Do it completely and thoroughly as a deliberate act of cutting yourself away from your past and moving into the present. As noted, your official record remains on file. However, you'll be taking steps to manage **how** and **when** you "Deliver the Mail" coming up in Chapter Eight.

Even after everything mentioned in this chapter and all the powerful reasons for removing yourself from the Internet, some challenged professionals will still be able to use (appropriately) some portion of their social media presence. If this applies to you, remember you will be competing head-to-head with others in your professional category that aren't challenged. Be mindful of the fact that you are not them; your situation is different. For you I recommend crafting a hybrid system using the *Get Beyond Your Troubled Past* approach and the New Job Search model. Build a strategy that gives you the qualified platform you need, without over-playing your hand. Above all, make sure your new persona is constructed using honesty and authenticity.

The Wrap-up

This chapter brings the first half of *Get Beyond Your Troubled Past* to a close. From here the backdrop, planning, and frame-of-mind concepts presented in the first six chapters will be applied. We'll begin with the nuts-n-bolts of job searching, applications, and résumés.

Action Steps

Practice being the receiver of your own message before sending it, knowing it's not what you intend that counts, rather it's all about how your message is received.

Put into practice these four "get along" tips for any situation:

- Know the norms of a particular environment

- Observe how others act in different situations

- Mirror the positive behaviors you see around you

- Act or change or adapt your behavior to blend in

Review your social media presence and apply the "less is more" rule.

Chapter Seven

Setting Up for Success

This chapter is about what you'll need to do and what you'll need to have before beginning your job search. You'll learn the best way to "Deliver the Mail" (your story) in an effective, positive, and honest way, so you're controlling the message rather than an employer finding out the truth at the worst time possible. Getting your story together is preparation for the upcoming chapters that lead you to the down-and-dirty, nitty-gritty of finding and retaining your initial Job Search Objective or JSO position.

Your Own Narrative

As you prepare to go out and actually meet people, you'll want to turn "your story" into a well-crafted background narrative. Your narrative is a tight, succinctly written version about the **what, how,** and **why** of your background snag. After reading and working through the tips and guidelines presented in the first six chapters of this book, you're ready to write your story. Many find this step cathartic, perhaps even therapeutic, and worth completing for this reason alone. For job searching purposes, writing how things came to be has a practical purpose, it helps pull your many "story pieces" together.

Consider doing this as the first step in constructing the "mail" you'll be delivering as you pursue your Job Search Objective or JSO. Do you remember my earlier taste of Delivering The Mail introduced in Chapter Five? It's your short, to the point, verbal communication with prospective employers about your situation. The finished product will be **The Mail** you actually deliver.

You may not find this assignment appealing, especially if you don't enjoy writing. Even so, I encourage you to do it anyway. What counts isn't grammar or sentence structure. It's all about your content. So relax, no one else has to see it. The purpose is to transfer the facts and circumstances of your story from your head to paper or your computer so you can **read it** versus **think it**.

Getting it out and down where you can read it, not only gives you a way to release some of what's built up over time, but it also helps clarify the facts. The act of reading what you write about you, back to you, removes the subconscious storyline you've probably used to support or defend your take on the situation. Remember, the Marketplace doesn't care how you feel about anything, your background problem included. For now, think of each prospective employer you meet as a stand-in for the Marketplace. As a result, you need a way to manage your message. Creating a background narrative gives you a way to manage the facts.

How to write it

You write your narrative in three separate sessions. Plan for at least two hours of work for session one. Pick a place and time when you won't be distracted or interrupted. Go to the library, a coffee shop, or whatever spot works for you. Sit down and begin writing, by hand or computer, it doesn't matter. Put your emphasis on getting your story out, not on the mechanics of writing and editing. Just write from the beginning and go straight through to the end in one sitting. The length depends on you; it might end up being four pages, seven pages, maybe a lot more. Just cover it all. Then put it away. Don't look at it again for at least three days; a week is even better.

During the second session, your task is to rewrite what you produced during the first session. Here's the kicker, you'll cut it in half. This means eliminate anything repetitive or otherwise not critical to your story. I know, it sounds tough, but do it anyway. Once it's done, put it away. Don't look at it for a few days. No peeking or tweaking allowed. Let it cool off so you can read it again with fresh eyes.

Haul out the second version of your story and, for session three, repeat step two. Rewrite and condense, cutting the length by half again. What remains is your basic narrative. Now you have the nuts-and-bolts of your story, the **what**, **how,** and **why** of your background problem.

Humans are hardwired to respond positively to stories, your story included. Your goal is to take **your sto**ry and turn it into **a story**. Your background narrative is about you; however, think of it as simply another tool in your job search tool bag. Your background narrative is the impersonal version of your original story. People who don't take this step find it hard to talk about their situation without rambling or becoming emotional. They don't understand how deeply they identify with their story, resulting in a version of it that can be counter-productive if not downright inappropriate.

Talking with a prospective employer isn't the time for a long, drawn out epic tale, nor is it the right time for an unstructured, jumbled rehash of your sad saga. The goal is delivering a condensed, edited version that aligns with your overall approach. Think back to the communication discussion in Chapter Six. What's vital is all about what's received by the other person, remember?

Delivering a well-crafted narrative requires, first, that you have one. Invest the time and effort to bring your story out of your head and into the open. Firm boundaries don't exist as long as your story stays in your mind. Writing helps you to separate fact from fiction. You can develop a tight, well thought-out narrative or story following these steps. This will result in a purposeful message about you, delivered by you, on your terms, at the time of your choosing.

Doing Your Own Criminal Background Check

In Chapter Four, I reviewed the process of cleaning up old business. In Chapter Six, I discussed the need to conduct a social media check. Both address problems and issues lurking just offstage. Usually these are different from the third discovery puzzle piece, your formal criminal record. If you've had encounters with law enforcement and the criminal justice system, you need a copy of your criminal report. Here's why.

First, you need to know what's on it. Even though you think you know your record, until you actually have a copy of it, you don't know for sure. As simple and basic as this seems, I'm continually amazed at how many people "think they know" what's there, but don't actually have a copy.

Second, you need to know what prospective employers will find when they do a background check on you. What you see and know must match with what they see and know. Why? Because you can't run the risk of being out of alignment, something I described in depth in the last chapter. Even more important, you'll need to disclose details of your criminal record on your application or at some point in your hiring process. If a discrepancy or omission is discovered, saying you didn't know won't cut it. You're expected to know, so make sure you do know.

Third, check your report for errors. The section below covers this in detail.

Getting your record

If all your reported criminal history took place within one state, I recommend going directly to that state to request your report. Do this by searching online. Just type in the name of the state followed by *"criminal history information,"* and follow the instructions. Expect to pay a fee, typically $20 to $40 per criminal record report.

If you know your reported activity took place in more than one state, do the same for each state. However, if you're uncertain which states, and, if you have any criminal history associated with a federal crime, go to www.fbi.gov and follow the instructions to get your FBI report. There's a cost to this, including a fee to get fingerprinted locally. But, just like with the state records, the fees are modest for something so important to reaching your goal.

You also have the option of using one of many firms providing background checks to consumers and businesses. The advantage of this option is speed. However, the accuracy of the information varies. So I recommend going to state or federal sources to get a copy of the most accurate, official record.

Reviewing your record for accuracy

When you receive your report, make a copy. This is your working copy, the one you'll mark up and highlight. File the original away along with other important papers. Report formats vary, so review your working copy line by line. Highlight any information you don't understand or that appears inaccurate. Listed here are some of things you should check, but don't limit it to only these points. Read and study every word and phrase.

- Name: Check for spelling, your correct middle initial or full middle name

- Social Security Number: Each time it appears on the report, check for accuracy

- Dates: Make sure they match your records or at least your recollection

- Penalty: Make sure the sentence listed matches the penalty you were given

- Disposition: Check to see charges and arrests conform to the actual outcomes (not guilty, case dismissed, sealed records, etc.)

None of this is intended to provide legal advice, same as the information you already read in Chapter Four about clearing up old business. Consider using a private attorney or Legal Aid to help weed through complicated, confusing reports. There are procedures available to correct errors using state and local resources.

If you choose to pursue fixing your record, start with the appropriate court in the jurisdiction associated with the error. Each jurisdiction, county, and state has their own procedure, so follow instructions carefully. If you need help, call or go in and get your record. Do you remember "The System" discussion in Chapter Four? Michael chose to be a worthy competitor using the rules, policies, and procedures of The System to achieve his objectives and so should you.

Here's another important point concerning your record. Carry a clean copy with you. In most cases, you won't need it; however, a situation might arise where producing a copy on the spot could be helpful. For example, if you've presented your background situation and the other person seems interested yet has questions, you can pull it out and say, "I realize you'll probably need to run your own report. For now, here's a copy of my official record." Make sure the report you carry is current and in good condition, not dog-eared, stained, or torn up. In fact, I recommend keeping it in a plastic sleeve.

Understand clearly, carrying this report is for you. It's only used if absolutely necessary. Consider the report as another tool and, like most tools, it remains in the bag until needed.

Steps Everyone Must Take

This next section reviews the steps every job seeker must take:

- Creating a résumé

- Completing job applications

- Communicating with employers about available jobs

I want you to see the products of these three steps (a résumé, an application, and an impression) in terms of elimination and not acceptance. In other words, the easiest way for an employer to remove candidates from consideration for a job is by using these basic steps. Each represents you. Take your finished application, for example. Applications come with instructions. If you can't or won't follow instructions and complete the application as requested, it's an easy, cost-effective elimination. Or, if the education or training requirements call for one type of certificate and you list a different certificate or nothing at all, the process stops.

The point is this; don't give potential employers **an easy reason to eliminate you** at this early stage of the hiring process. This means follow instructions in detail regarding the steps of the process. Provide all information as requested. You will learn in Chapter Eight that I consider applications, résumés, and follow-up communication as part of an overall job search process, one that places the greatest emphasis on personal contact. Don't expect to attract or wow an employer by your application or résumé alone.

Consider them as part of the supporting cast of necessary puzzle parts that on their own won't take you to stardom, but can sink you if done incorrectly.

The last ten years

To prepare for building your résumé and filling out applications, you'll need a list of where you've lived and worked in the past. The first question that pops into most people's heads is, "How far back?" There's no clear-cut answer to this question because it's determined mostly by the information you're asked to provide on the applications you haven't completed yet. I recommend starting with the last ten years.

You also need this information for creating your résumé, but not in as much detail. Your résumé is your document, so you have flexibility in how it's created. Applications, on the other hand, are inflexible. They can be basic and off-the-shelf, or complex and unique to one employer exclusively. However, all applications require details including dates, addresses, phone numbers, email addresses, and names.

If you're fortunate, you'll have most of this information. If so, great, just bring it up to date and you're ready to move forward. If not, do your best to sort out what you have. Then, starting with today's date, list in reverse order, where you've worked and lived for the last ten years. I recommend doing this on a computer using an outline format that will make editing much easier. If you prefer to do this longhand, skip lines and give yourself plenty of room to include things you remember later.

Whether you're just updating an existing list or putting one together from easy-to-assemble documents, the goal is creating a master document that lists where you've lived and worked during the last ten years. When complete, especially if you've done the work using a computer, it's a short hop to add your education, training, and experiences that come to mind as you repeatedly review your list. If you can go longer than ten years, absolutely do it. Remember to save or copy all your work. I suggest emailing it to yourself as a way to save and store this information. If you have to do this again in the future, you'll have it and only need to bring it up to the current date.

Don't skip this step because you'll have to do it anyway when you fill out detailed job applications. Digging, sorting, and piecing it all together as you're trying to complete an application can set you off on the wrong path. Even with your list, you may have overlooked something, or you didn't anticipate you'd need something and you must look for that one thing. Imagine having to look for and re-create everything as you're working on an application that's already demanding enough to complete.

Take it step by step to reduce the "hassle factor" and to increase your accuracy. Making time to pull your list together before starting your first job application is something you'll thank yourself for later.

Job applications

A job application starts as a document owned by the employer. But ownership changes once you sign and submit it. For the background-challenged applicant, this is a key point. You own what you submit. Applications can live on in paper and digital form for a long time. Before you even consider filling out an application keep the following in mind:

- You own it

- You signed it

- You stated it was accurate

- You can expect it to live on for years

Completing job applications is time consuming and draining, physically and emotionally. This is especially true for long, overly inclusive online applications that are like black holes, sucking up your time and energy. Here's the good news:

Don't ...

invest one minute ...

filling out an application for a job ...

that doesn't fit your JSO or align with your Five-year Plan.

Period.

Your time and energy are too precious to waste but that's exactly what'll happen if you fill out and submit applications out of alignment with your JSO.

Okay, so what's the bad news? The applications you complete must be close to perfect. Again, a job application itself won't get you a job but, if done poorly, it can prevent you from getting one. Furthermore, you own it, signed it, agreed it's accurate, and you know it'll be around for years. So, be selective. Choose only those jobs that fit your JSO, and be picky about how you complete it—no blanks, no winging it, no sloppiness. Answer every question fully and accurately. When given an opportunity to "add more information" don't under-explain and don't over-explain.

As you'll only submit applications for positions in alignment with your JSO and Five-year Plan, you won't have to complete as many applications as you think. Forget stories of people submitting hundreds of applications with no results. Whatever they're doing doesn't apply to you. You're the one who chooses whether to apply or not. So, choose wisely and carefully. And remember, being truthful and honest isn't optional, it's mandatory.

Before moving on to résumés, here are a few application tips:

- Read the instructions—for the entire application and for completing each section.

- Complete all of it, let nothing slip, and leave nothing blank.

- Review your work for readability and check for correct spelling.

- Keep it tight and on topic. Avoid carrying, embellishing, or trying to impress if given the opportunity to "tell us more." My rule of thumb is, when given the option to add additional information, shoot for an added ten percent by highlighting key areas, just enough to create interest and no more.

- If you need it, ask for help from a tech-savvy friend to upload your résumé or any other requested documents. Keep notes for later use on how it was done.

- This is important. At the beginning of your search, select a position to apply for with an extensive application you can save and print. Try hard to find one that fits your JSO and Plan. However, for this instance only, stretch a little beyond your JSO (**only** if needed) to find a great application. Take your time completing it, saving it, and returning to it as necessary to insure everything is correct and complete. When you're finished, print a copy for yourself to use as a template when filling out other applications. I recommend carrying a copy with you along with a copy of your criminal record, if applicable, as you physically move about introducing yourself, interviewing with people, and following up.

Before shifting to our discussion about résumés, there's something critical I must address—it's the "Ban The Box Initiative." In an attempt to restrict the use of criminal history questions on employment applications, a number of states and municipalities around the country have introduced or passed ordinances restricting use of the criminal record check-box.

Right now, there's substantial momentum for these changes. However, we're still in the early stages and there's little to go on regarding how it will play out, especially when it comes to private employers. As significant and important as this subject is, attempts to find solutions through legislation and litigation progress at a snail's pace. If you successfully move past the application phase due to no check-box, fabulous; this book will assist you in completing your job search effectively. Regardless of how all of this turns out, keep in mind that you are an independent Free Agent, operating in the open Marketplace. Stay a heads-up player, use every tool available to you, and don't relinquish the responsibility of achieving your objectives to anyone.

Constructing your résumé

One of the most dreaded parts of searching for a job is constructing a résumé. This is particularly true if you're creating one from scratch. Even people who enjoy expressing themselves through writing can find it a tough assignment.

People wrangle with putting together résumés because it's a creative endeavor. Not everyone's experienced with or "wired for" creative writing. Good résumé writing comes from the same neighborhood as advertising copy writing, which is different from journalism and book reports. Complicating things further, a résumé is a document about you, made by you. Many people have a hard time writing or talking about themselves, especially in an unabashed, self-promotional way. There's an entire industry built around and intertwined with résumés, including:

- Résumé writers

- Recruiters and head hunters

- Software packages (ATS – applicant tracking systems)

- Job coaches and more

The stakes seem high, and they can be, depending on the situation. But the fact is that the résumé, like the job application, has become an elimination tool for those doing the hiring. What started out as a summary of qualifications has become a mix of art and spy craft where look-and-feel designs convey subtle messages and key words are embedded to penetrate ATS screens and firewalls.

This spy-vs-spy résumé environment is so far off the mark for many background-challenged seekers, it's absurd, especially if the background problem is significant and the amount of time away from the job market is extensive. The whole résumé area is way over-hyped, adding confusion and difficulty when it comes to putting a résumé together that actually works for you.

So, let's take the subject back down to the ground floor, because the complexity and sophistication of ATS-enhanced résumés starts off way too high. Don't get me wrong, this isn't because you're less worthy, it's because the current state of résumé affairs has evolved from the old click-and-send method where hundreds of résumés and cover letters were blasted out. Although the New Job Search approach referred to in Chapter Six is more about being found than chasing and pursuing, there's a shared origin, the Internet. Your situation is different. Your background issues present two problems you must overcome.

First, you and your background issues are fairly easy to spot. Therefore, assume you'll be screened out early in the process via application and résumé review. This is a Marketplace function, and it's just how it is. So, accept it as neither fair nor unfair. It's just the rules of the game, which you understand like everyone else.

Second, if you progress deep into the hiring process, there's a real danger of becoming emotionally over-invested in obtaining a position you won't land. Your energy, time, and enthusiasm will be burned up and your attention will be concentrated on one opportunity to the exclusion of other possibilities. When working to secure your initial job the odds of being successful increase if you see yourself as a baseball hitter that goes to the plate trying for a single or double, not a home run.

The best approach for you is to focus on your JSO, working your plan, and meeting people. It's not about blasting out résumés or setting up a polished social media persona as the best way to be found and recruited. It's my belief your background problem renders most Internet-based methods counter-productive. This is so for the vast majority of challenged seekers. Yes, of course, I know there are always exceptions to the rule. That's fine. Remember, I live in Las Vegas, so I've come to appreciate the value of knowing the odds of the game.

Keeping things simple, your résumé should

- Market you effectively

- Communicate about you

- Align with and support your JSO

Marketing you effectively

Your résumé is your marketing document, your business card, and brochure all rolled into one. As such, it's an important job-search tool. But don't over-think this. When an actual human being reviews a stack of résumés, each gets about the same amount of time it takes to sip a cup of coffee. That's it.

It must be neat, clean, and crisp with no folds, wrinkles, or stains. There should be no spelling or grammatical errors either, because your résumé represents you. Little flaws like this will eliminate you immediately. If your résumé is messy, it translates as you're messy.

It also must be easy to read or scan quickly. You'll be presenting it to a potential customer, your prospective employer. A fundamental rule of thumb for you as the seller is to make it easy for your customer to buy. I'm serious. If you hand over a chock-full, busy, overly detailed résumé with tiny, weird fonts, tell me, who'll struggle through reading it?

Your résumé must present you in a positive, appropriate manner. Positive means you say nice things about yourself and your abilities. Appropriate indicates those things align with what an employer is looking for in a new employee. Remember, don't over-complicate the résumé subject. Keep it simple, positive, and focused.

Communicate about you

Okay, here's a bubble buster. Let's assume your résumé touches on all the expected areas, has a nice layout, and is clean and error free. Aside from your name, what's the most important piece of information on your résumé? Drum roll please ... **your phone number**.

Keep in mind **your** résumé doesn't exist to appeal to the automated key word scanning systems. Its function is assisting you in appealing to and communicating with another person. Let's assume this is a busy human, one who looks over your résumé between bites of their sandwich, as the phone rings, and people pop in and out of his or her office with all kinds of requests. Picture this person taking the time to respond to you by email or, better yet, typing or writing something to you via snail mail. Come on; get real. If they're interested, either they or someone working for them will pick up the phone and call you.

That's it. In basic, simple terms, the purpose of your résumé is to induce and facilitate the call. Therefore, make sure your phone number is correct and easy to read. When they call, answer in a mature, professional manner. You're on a job search. I hope you understand, "Hey ...," or "Wass-up ...?" doesn't quite fit, right?

There's a good chance the call will go to your voice-mail. Plan for this and record a message in your own voice, using your name, something like, "Hi, this is Andy, please leave your name and number, and I'll return your call as soon as I can." Keep it short, **pleasant**, and easy to understand, containing no background noise or your "signature" music.

Please, get it together when it comes to recording your message. When a prospective employer calls you, what they hear (your words, your actual voice, and the message you have recorded) are direct reflections of you. Remember, it's not what you think or intend that counts, it's what and how it's received.

When searching for a job, see your phone as a business device first and a social device second. Make sure to check and clear voice mail messages **at least** twice a day. How ridiculous would it be, after all you've done to reach the point of receiving an employer's call, only to miss it because you didn't check or had a full inbox? Also, make certain you have minutes available, which means, you may have to make changes with how you use your phone. Employers will contact you by phone, expect it, and be ready for it.

This reminds me of one of my favorite quotes attributed to legendary football coach Vince Lombardi. He said, "Son, when you get to the end zone, act like you've been there before." Prepare for **the call** and control your communication, in advance! Make it nice and easy for your "customer" to get through, leave you a message, and have a smooth, professional experience along the way.

Aligning with your JSO

I don't encourage the idea of adjusting your résumé to suit different job opportunities. You shouldn't have to do this because you should be pursuing **only positions that match your JSO**. For the most part, I feel your energy is better spent working your plan and the overall process, not tweaking your résumé. Small adjustments to the layout or content may be needed once you start searching, this is normal. But tailoring to suit individual opportunities or frequent overhauls of your entire document isn't a smart idea.

There are hundreds of books out there on résumés. Lots of great material exists on the subject. Check the resource section of my website for recommendations. Consider the points below when selecting your résumé style. Always err on the side of simplicity and clarity. As I've stated, your résumé alone won't get you hired. View it as your marketing document and another tool, created to serve a specific purpose: **to achieve your JSO**. Here's what to keep in mind when writing your résumé:

- Limit it to one page, centered

- Use one font type, 10-12 point Arial, Times New Roman, Courier, or similar

- Keep the formatting simple and consistent using bold, italics, and underlining only

- Print on standard white copier paper

- Align the content of your résumé to connect with your JSO

- Use either a chronological approach or a skills-based format—don't use a work history "laundry list" approach when creating your résumé

Construct your résumé using five sections:

1. Title: name, address, email address, phone number

2. Objective: your actual JSO or a statement summarizing it

3. Work Experience: paid and unpaid work-related experience

137

4. Education: Training and service, giving priority to training related to your JSO

5. References: Include the full name and phone numbers of three people other than family. Get permission first and make sure the numbers are correct and working.

Again, there's a vast amount of résumé material available and many highly creative and capable résumé specialists working in the field. I realize my overall approach and suggestions may seem basic, simplistic, and perhaps rather old-school in style. I understand. Even so, **my goal is to shrink down the profile of your résumé**, to fit it in the tool box, and give it a purpose:

To Serve Your JSO!

Frankly, some people need an old-fashioned, objective-toting résumé to stay on track. For them, it's a good idea to start each job-searching day by reading the top third of their résumé. They need reminding of what they're out to accomplish to prevent loss of focus and veering off course. It's the question they begin each day asking. The answer is always the same, and it's **right there on their résumé**.

If your goal was appealing to the digital world in the form of an automated tracking system, I'm in favor of something different. But it's not. This applies to everyone with background issues, former professionals included. Regardless of their prior experience using sophisticated and competitive résumés, my advice is the same, appeal first to a person and second (or not at all) to the digital world.

This may be a hard pill to swallow. You might be getting lots of counsel to the contrary. My response is this; imagine how swift and cold your next fall will be when you've hooked your wagon to the digital universe instead of people. Yes, I know, working with real people is challenging. Still, the truth is no online website or digitized job application will speak on your behalf or carry water for you. Trust me; working with real people is a requirement to achieve your JSO and all other significant mile markers en route to reaching your Five-year Goal.

The Wrap-up

Each of the characters in this book initially used a simple, skill-based résumé format that aligned with their JSO. They were coached to understand their first task was to meet people through introduction and the résumé came second. They were taught that their résumé was their primary marketing document **but** they understood it was one of many tools in their job search tool bag. Each followed my résumé game plan meticulously and it worked.

In the next chapter, we'll get down to the business of actually searching for your first critical position. We'll discuss introductions, communication, the how-to of Delivering The Mail and interviewing. I'm excited to finally get down to it, so buckle up and let's plunge ahead together.

Action Steps

Write and edit your personal narrative.

Conduct your own background check.

Prepare your Ten-year List.

Find and complete an application template.

Create your simple effective résumé.

Chapter Eight

Getting Your First Job

This chapter takes us to where the rubber finally meets the road, your actual job search. Your goal is achieving your Job Search Objective (JSO) using a sales-based approach as introduced in Chapter Five. In this chapter, I'll show you how to put everything you've done up until now into practice. Like any other capable salesperson, you need to know where to direct your efforts. This begins with knowing where not to look.

Where Not to Look

Okay, it's time for a disclaimer. Nothing's cut in stone here. My way of going about this is certainly not the only way. The problem is that most other ways are geared toward helping people without background issues. It's easy to miss this point due to the sheer volume of material out there to accommodate the majority—those people with nothing of consequence in their background.

Years ago, it became apparent to me that just **getting a job** for a background-challenged person isn't the biggest concern. What's important is getting one connected to a greater goal. Over the years, after working with hundreds of clients, I saw a crying need for building business and personal relationships that help transcend the unending barriers inevitably created by major background problems. Over time, I developed my approach, which works exceedingly well when it's understood and followed.

Las Vegas, where I live and work, provides a perfect example. What I'm about to describe happens frequently, especially when a job seeker goes after a position cold, without a personal recommendation from someone already working for the employer with the available job. Plus, if he or she is grasping at straws by taking a shot at a position that doesn't fit a defined JSO, odds are the job seeker will get nowhere fast.

Let's make this more interesting and assume this person is you. For years you wanted to work for one of the major hotel casino groups on the famous Las Vegas Strip. In spite of your major felony and clue-ridden, choppy work history, you decide you're just as deserving as others, so why not give it a shot? Perhaps you've even heard some major hotel groups hire ex-offenders, in fact a few may even have **ex-offender programs**. You forge ahead.

For discussion purposes, let's say you make it over the first hurdle and are asked to come in for "an interview." Great. You book a time and add it to your calendar. On the appointment day, you scrub up, dress appropriately, and drive over to the property. After parking and a very long walk, you arrive at the HR department, where you check in. While waiting, you take the opportunity to review your application using one of their computers. At last, it's your turn. However, the conversation with the fresh, young screener takes only a couple of minutes and it's over. She sends you off with a cheery, "Thanks for coming in. We'll review your application and get back to you."

Chances are it ends there. You invested application and travel time, as well as emotional capital, and now it's all out the window. If you're one of the few who gets past the screener, you can expect to waste more time going to a next-level interview, which you won't pass.

How to know you aren't getting anywhere

First off, a major employer with an HR hiring process that's more than a few people thick is an opportunity-killer for you. What aren't you getting here? If your application itself doesn't weed you out, the screener will. If you get beyond him or her, your chances of success decrease significantly with each level up. Think about it. You're competing with others that most likely have zero background problems. Their experience, education, and training are made to order for the position. Unlike you, these people aren't "taking a shot" at something because the job they're pursuing matches perfectly with their JSO.

Second, remember you're looking for a person first, not a job. How many people do you actually get to introduce yourself to by applying this time- and energy-wasting route? The person who "interviewed" you during the screening has a job to perform. That job is to screen you out, not befriend you. If it was Becky Sue for example, she's been trained well and is good at her job. Perhaps this whole experience was new to you. You went in thinking you would actually meet someone who mattered. In fact, there was virtually no chance this would happen.

The front end of this type of hiring process, including the application, the initial appointment, and the screening interview itself, are tasks right out of the virtual Las Vegas HR On-boarding Manual. It's stored in a well-traveled part of the Marketplace and shared by most large hotel casino operators. They know what they want and in most cases, unfortunately, they don't want you. This isn't because they're mean, horrible people. That's hardly true. In fact, they're professionals all competing in the Marketplace.

They're experienced and heads-up about people and the liabilities background issues can bring to their organizations. So, they pick and choose accordingly. After all, it's business.

Take a moment and give this truth a little quality thought. What's in it for a large employer to hire you? There's no one on the inside recommending you and other candidates may be a better fit from the standpoint of experience, education, and training. To top it off, you have bumps, perhaps big bumps including a money crime, in your background.

Do you think large employers hang out a sign saying they're interested or not interested in certain types or categories of people? For example: short, fat people need not apply. Really? How about: felons, addicts, or people suffering from major depression need not apply. Of course not. Look, any employer (especially large ones) can be expected to do what's in their best interest. This is a time-honored Marketplace rule. If there's another equally qualified, yet "less complicated" person available, they'll hire them over you. I know, this is **their perspective**, but for your purposes, it's the only one that matters.

Even with all this knowledge, I can hear you now, "*Yeah, but they were nice and seemed interested.*"

Okay, so? They won't tell you anything because **they can't tell you anything**. Becky Sue's got a job to do. She's evaluated regularly on how well she does it. The last thing she'll do is jeopardize her position by not following the company policy.

I hope this is clear because you can't afford to run around charging at windmills. There are Marketplace rules and you must know them to avoid burning yourself out on extremely low percentage long shots. Your mission is to work your plan, establish a foothold for yourself, and dig in. My mission is to tell you the truth, even if it's a little unpleasant at times. Every ounce of energy spent "off objective" or thinking "it won't matter" is energy lost.

Where not to look

Here's a major tip, knowing where **not to look** is half the battle. Once you've removed all that doesn't apply from consideration and align with what does apply, searching will become easier to grasp and far more straightforward. I'm describing the flipside of your JSO, which exists to guide you toward your objective. Consider for a moment, it's also in place to steer you away from everything else. Your JSO tells you at a glance what to go after and **what to not go after**. It gives you a solid reason and permission to pass any "We're Hiring" signs with nothing whatsoever to do with you or your JSO. All job seekers should avoid positions out of alignment with what they are out to achieve, but it goes double for everyone with background blemishes.

Then, there's the issue of your Personal Job One, or PJO. Remember? We discussed it in Chapter Two. It's your big underlying life challenge that must be managed to have any real chance of ongoing success. Imagine reaching for something outside your Job Search Objective that's in conflict with your PJO.

For example, imagine the repeat offender rejected by the big employer who goes looking for sympathy and support in old familiar places and faces, or the sober alcoholic who somehow thinks it's different this time and doesn't eliminate bars from his list. How about a recovering drug addict who knows exactly where the jobs and worksites are that can create compromising situations, but plows ahead anyway. Or, imagine someone battling mental health issues who's considering an overly high-stress, fast-paced environment? Circumstances that haven't worked out for you in the past are certainly not where you want to be again.

Avoiding these situations seems like obvious, absolute no-brainers. Just wait until things take off in real time. Amnesia, confusion, or doubts can all set in, resulting in maneuvers that are way off the map. In fact, they're so far off the map; it would be funny if it wasn't so serious. No one's exempt, not even you **Mr. or Ms. Professional**. Egos can be demanding just like addictions, propelling even the former professional to do things they swore, way back, at their lowest moments, they would never, ever do again.

My experience helping hundreds of clients with this aspect of job searching has firmed up my point of view in a major way. In fact, my position has solidified, even though openness and flexibility are two attributes that make me highly successful at what I do to help people. As a background-challenged person, you must focus your efforts. Thinking you can't afford **not** to consider all options is like an airplane trying to take flight backwards; it doesn't work and never will. You may end up somewhere, but just "getting somewhere" isn't your goal. Add to this the clock is ticking and your financial, physical, and emotional resources are limited.

You must be picky and resist any impulse to pull back from a narrow job search. "After all," you may reason, "I have so many limitations already. I have to consider everything and anything, just to get **any** job." This is a big mistake.

Eliminating options that don't apply to you should be a major concern. For one thing, it relieves you of thinking you must charge in every direction at once. Like the Shotgun Approach in Chapter Three, trying to cover all the bases turns into something completely counter-productive. Eliminating options also brings you clarity. You'll see quickly and definitively, this option fits and that one doesn't. Removing possibilities that don't align with your JSO is like clearing away gray clouds that block your view. When you do, the road ahead is better understood.

This brings Michael to mind again. Before getting his initial position at Arnie's, which aligned perfectly with his JSO, Michael went on a wild, roller coaster ride of indecision and impatience. One week he was on top, focused on his JSO. The next week he was plunging downward into the abyss, frazzled and disconnected. I met him at Starbucks one afternoon, following a hard day job searching. It wasn't an "on top day."

Michael Pulls Out of the Trenches

"Wow! Michael it looks like you've had quite a day!" I said. One glance communicated volumes. Michael fidgeted, half in and half out of his chair, trying with little success to position his bag, phone, and white and green coffee cup on the small table. He wore brown slacks and what had been a nicely pressed, rust-colored shirt in the morning. Now his shirt was rumpled and hung loosely about his frame. He pulled an overflowing folder out of his bag. I had no trouble spotting a Craigslist printout for a security guard position.

"Yeah, right. Quite a day. Yesterday, too," he said without making eye contact.

I took a sip of coffee giving him a moment to settle in and catch up. "I haven't seen you in a week. Bring me up to speed, how's the search going?"

"I don't know, okay I guess ...." He paused, took a deep breath, and flipped both hands up in the air. "Ya know, I'm not sure sticking with this one thing is the best way to go. I mean, I've been talking with Mo. He says a couple of guys got hired as security guards; one has a background just like mine. I don't know, maybe I should think about that." Michael leaned forward, cocking his head slightly to the right, giving me his serious, street face.

Mo (or Maurice) was one of his home boys from the old neighborhood. Unlike Michael, he'd managed to avoid problems with the police and The System. However, Mo was still rooted in the environment that contributed to Michael's difficulties. Mo somehow avoided getting tangled up with the law while Michael paid his debt to society and now was saddled with background issues.

"I noticed," I said, pointing to the Craigslist ad. "What else have you gone after?"

Michael opened the folder and an array of job postings spilled out. He gestured to the pile.

"How's that working out for you?" I asked as Michael sat silent.

"How many different kind of job applications have you filled out?" Again, no response from the sullen Michael.

"Look, if you want to be a security guard, that's fine," I said. "But it's not what you told me, and it's not what it says on your résumé. Help me out, what's going on? What happened to last week's enthusiasm about the job with Applebee's and the one at Arnie's?"

"They're both still possible, but I can't keep waiting around. I have to get something going fast. Ya know what I mean, John?"

I didn't reply. I'd been here before with Michael. He wanted to argue about why sticking to his JSO wasn't in his best interest. He was looking for reasons to listen to Mo and do what other guys were doing instead. But he wouldn't get it from me, because it wasn't mine to give. If Michael decided to switch up or abandon his JSO simply because Mo said someone else got hired as a security guard, he'd be turning his boat crossways into the Marketplace wind. He'd end up jumping from one lily pad to another lily pad and he knew it.

"It's your decision, Michael. If you think listening to Mo, which I'll remind you is anything but being proactive, is in your best interest, you make the call. You know where I stand."

We finished our coffee, talking about his sister and mother. Michael got the call for an interview at Arnie's two days later. The subject of a security guard job for him never came up again.

148

Your Sales-based Approach

Let's start with a little review. Here's where you'll find yourself if you've followed the steps I've outlined in the chapters so far. You understand you're a Free Agent competing in the Marketplace. It's clear placing all your eggs in the digital basket doesn't address your needs. You have a Five-year Plan and a more immediate Job Search Objective (JSO). You've cleaned up old business, taken steps to manage your online profile and, if applicable, secured a copy of your criminal record. Also, you understand living in the past and worrying about the future are counter-productive. And that it's up to you to stay focused and operating in the present. With work history and résumé in hand and your knowledge of where not to look, you're ready to start searching.

Here's where the selling part comes into play. Selling your service to an employer is like any other sales process, it involves steps. There are big advantages to using steps. Let me highlight a couple of significant ones:

- First, there's a built-in sequence to the steps. You start with #1, complete it, then move to #2, complete it, and so on. The order doesn't change, and you don't need to re-think each move, with every job possibility.

- Second, the order and sequence help you know where you stand with each potential job. This is important because mid-way through the process of achieving your JSO, you'll be working on lots of opportunities simultaneously. However, they won't all be at the same step. Using steps and documenting where you're at with each step is critical to staying on top of everything happening.

- Job search steps will become your best friend. At any point during the hectic, tiring days to come, you can stop and remind yourself what you should be doing with any given job possibility. Knowing which step you're on is crucial because it tells you exactly what you should do next: **Move the process to the next step.**

Moving on to the Next Step

There are seven steps in the job search process. They're uncomplicated and easy to follow, but don't underestimate the value of each one. My challenge to you is to use them, stick to them, and to know which step you're on with each job opportunity. I don't want you to wonder or worry about what your next move should be in the process. The answer is always the same, to move each opportunity to the next step.

- Step One – Your Introduction

- Step Two – Present Your Résumé

- Step Three – Make Application

- Step Four – Follow-up Number One

- Step Five – Follow-up Number Two

- Step Six – An Interview with a Decision Maker

- Step Seven – Make the Sale & You Get Hired

Let's take a careful look at each one.

Step one – your introduction

Notice that Step One is Your Introduction and not Make Application. You already have a Plan and a JSO and you know where not to look. Here's a reminder: If it doesn't align with your JSO, you don't look there, period. You know blasting off résumés and investing lots of time applying for jobs out of alignment, is a waste, a downer, and a pain. Last but certainly not least, you know you're looking to find a person not just a job because it takes real people to help you over the barriers created by your background issues.

So, where do you start? The answer is with **an introduction**. This is a way of meeting someone for the first time. For your purposes, introductions come in two forms: those initiated by a third person and those initiated by you. Here's where the power of your JSO comes into play. Your introduction is the vehicle you use to **share** with another person **what you want**. Notice I use the word "share." I could've used the word "tell" but that's too much of a one-way street.

For example, you share your JSO and then ask for the other person's input and ideas. They give it and you listen. They may ask for clarification. If so, restate your JSO. They might offer suggestions on other JSOs for you. When this happens, you politely reply, "Thank you, but no." Stick with your JSO. A made-up mind is a powerful force. Next, ask again for suggestions, recommendations, and referrals. At this point, clearly the other person understands what you're out to accomplish. Your role from then on is to be a good listener.

Third party introductions

A third party introduction is simply one arranged for or done by, another person. Here's how you get them. You share with everyone you know, "My objective is to work (your JSO goes here). Who can you introduce me to or recommend I speak with, about achieving my objective?"

Let me repeat, because this one slips by some people; **share this with everyone you know**. No beating around the bush, start by doing this. No holding back, no one is overlooked. You have a JSO and you must share it with people **asking** for introductions, referrals, and suggestions. How else will they come to you? Don't expect other people to read your mind or "just know" what you want. Share, then ask. When they reply, your job is to listen and then do the following:

- **Clarify anything** you didn't catch or follow completely. Hint: This is where you write it down, right in front of the person so you don't forget it. Doing this also shows you care and will follow up right away on their suggestions or referrals. After all, can you give other people any bigger compliment? With your actions, you're saying. *"What you're giving me is so important, I'm writing it down, right here, right now."*

- Thank them.

- Move on it. You just received a lead so take action immediately. Don't wait. Don't mull it over. Just move ahead as if you're on autopilot because amazing stuff happens when you put things in motion.

Self-introductions

These are introductions you line up yourself. They come in two flavors.

First, are the introductions pointed directly at an employer with no one in-between. For example, you're a talented graphic designer and you spot a graphic design business, so you walk in and introduce yourself. It's as simple as that.

Second, are the introductions that are purposefully indirect. Let's say your JSO is finding a position as a shipping and receiving specialist. So you ask a couple of truck drivers for the name of the Dock Supervisor. Once you have it, you walk in and ask to speak with that person.

Look, I know what you're thinking, "Yeah, but this ...," and "Yeah, but that ...." I get it, you hate doing this because it takes effort and you might get rejected. **Get over it**.

Here's another tip: the strongest leads you'll ever get are the ones you develop yourself. Take note of the word "develop." Regardless of how you get to the point of introducing yourself, it's ultimately up to you to put and keep the ball in motion. You're fitting the pieces together and taking action. I call this "development." Accept it, own it, and keep the momentum moving forward in a positive direction.

Employment services

A visit to your local employment service starts with you walking in and introducing yourself to an employment representative. What separates you from the nearly every other background-challenged person is your JSO. You'll use it **right in your introduction**. That's way different compared to how most other people they talk with every day, operate. Additionally, you're prepared to hold firm to your JSO. Be mindful that the representative you talk with may have their own agenda. For example, after talking with you and reviewing your paperwork, they might see you filling a position they need filled. That would be good except it probably doesn't match your JSO. Their agenda isn't your agenda and their problem certainly isn't your problem. You're there to receive leads that turn into introductions **in alignment with your JSO**. That's it, no change, no deviation. If what they offer isn't in alignment, don't drift off course. Thank them, get their card, and check back in a few days to see if they have something else that suits your needs.

Okay, let's give the job center representative the benefit of the doubt. Let's assume your approach is refreshing because it allows him or her to get down to business. Too many people show up with a totally reactive, "What do you have for me?" mindset. How nice for the representative to meet you. You're like a breath of fresh air, a person who actually knows what they want and who communicates it in a straight-up, crystal clear manner.

How to work an introduction

The bottom line question to consider as you approach an introduction is: are you fully in alignment? Are you and your JSO in sync? As you prepare for your immediate task of presenting your JSO, stay on your toes when it comes to alignment. Then get to the point quickly and share with the other person why you're there. Remember to listen to what they share with you in return. Your goal is **to move the process to the next of the seven steps**. It's like moving the ball down the field until a score is made. In this case, when a job is offered, you just scored.

Step two – present your résumé

What's the next step? It's Step Two, presenting your résumé. Do it subtly. For example, if the other person responds, "There's nothing available," here's an excellent way to play it. Thank them and pull a "Columbo." Columbo was a TV detective series back in the 1970s. The detective, played by Peter Falk, would start moving away as if he was finished with the conversation. Then he'd come back quickly with another little question to move the investigation forward. For you it might be something like, "Oh, by the way, may I leave a copy of my résumé?" Reach out, hand it over, and then step back slightly with a smile. Occasionally, a person won't reach back for it. But if you do it right, they'll walk away with a copy of your résumé in hand. Now, you've just accomplished Step Two. Remember, practice always makes perfect.

Step three – make application

Step Three is making application. At times, you'll do it earlier in the process, but shoot for making application as your third step in the journey. This was covered in Chapter Seven. Take a minute to flip back and review that section now.

Note: At some point in this seven-step process, you'll Deliver The Mail (DTM). This could happen during step one (your introduction) but mostly likely it'll happen during one of your two follow-ups. I don't recommend waiting until the interview for you to DTM, though, on occasion, it can happen this way. You'll find the discussion about this later in this chapter just after Step Seven.

Steps four and five – follow-up one and two

Steps Four and Five are the same: follow-up. **The most important thing about following up is to do it**. Most people have trouble doing it once and very few do it twice. So place yourself ahead of nearly every other person out there job searching by actually accomplishing both steps. Whenever possible do your follow-ups in person.

Each time you follow-up

- Remain consistently in alignment with your JSO

- Be polite and brief with the people you talk to each time

- Ask for suggestions and recommendations from them

- Express thanks and appreciation for their time

Keep in mind these are business steps, not personal steps. Situations change quickly in the business world and few things are ever "completely over" in an absolute way. There may be nothing available with a particular employer at the moment, but what about tomorrow? Next month? Next year? Many times I've seen an employer's first choice not work out, resulting in a call my client receives because they remained consistent, patient, and in alignment with every contact.

Please understand this, following up gives you a chance to show others how you roll each and every time. It's easy for people to be focused and on task—once. What about twice, three times, every time? If you stay in the follow-up zone, you'll develop your own opportunities simply because others will see for themselves that you're consistent and unwavering.

Step six – an interview with a decision maker

Here comes the big one: Step Six, Interviewing. As with résumés, there's an endless supply of resources with suggestions, tips, and the "how to" for acing an interview. Keep in mind **the interview is just one step in the process**. Weigh it as no more and no less important than the other six steps. Placing less emphasis on any of the earlier steps increases the chances you won't reach Step Six.

It's time for another tip. Your secret goal is securing a position without a formal interview. This can happen when you nail every other step so well, there's no need for the traditional "make it or break it" interview.

Getting hired without an interview is more likely to happen with smaller businesses, or one experiencing rapid change or growth. As a job seeker methodically working your steps, you'll never know everything going on behind the curtain. How could you know what appeared to be a slow, semi-responsive hiring process was actually caused by a management promotion? A lapse in time happened before the ball was handed off. Now there's a new manager in charge. They're behind and need to catch up. From the new manager's perspective, you're showing up at exactly the right time even though you've been at it well before they burst upon the scene. Suddenly, you're zipped to the front of the line, in spite of your background, because the new manager is under pressure to ramp things up quickly. I've seen this and similar scenarios in action. Nothing's over until it's over, so follow the game plan laid out for you in this book.

You may not generally think along these lines; however, interviews come in several varieties. Consider each contact with a potential employer as a possible interview. For example, the tour you get of the back of the shop or office may be your interview. Or, you're asked to come back and you end up waiting. How you handle yourself in the reception area could be your interview. Or, you may be observed by Mrs. Sampson, the office administrator, during your many comings and goings. Robert, the owner, always asks Mrs. Sampson what she thinks because she's always right and he hates interviewing anyway. If you blow off Mrs. Sampson, you're done without even knowing it. So, don't slack off or drop your focus, consider each visit and each interaction like an interview.

In most cases, there will be a formal interview. Keep the following in mind as you prepare for and go in for an interview. Here's what to remember on every interview:

- Be on time. Check/test your driving route a couple days ahead to make sure.

- Bring extra copies of your résumé along with all the other materials you usually carry when job searching. Frequently, someone unexpected will pop in, and it's helpful if you can supply them with a résumé on the spot.

- Be appropriate and in alignment. *Look*, *act*, *smell*, and *be* the part.

- Be polite. Take your lead from the person(s) conducting the interview. This is one time and place where being reactive is expected and appropriate.

- Smile and make eye contact with each person on the interview team, especially as the questions and conversation move from one person to another.

- Answer every question fully and briefly. A big reason people bomb when they're interviewed is because they fail to answer the question asked of them.

- Ask questions to clarify what they're looking for if you need to before answering.

Most important of all, when being interviewed, make sure you're authentically you. This is achieved by doing. You "show" who you are by behaving in an honest and straight-up way that's fully in alignment with your JSO.

Again, consider interviewing as another step in the process. Your job is to **take each step seriously**, moving the process to the next and final step, making a sale of your services to an employer.

Most people need the actual practice of interviewing to improve their skills. In practical terms, this means it takes three to five interviews before achieving your initial JSO. Shoot for three interviews. If it happens sooner, that's terrific. If it takes more than five interviews, you may need to regroup. In any case, applying yourself to the approach offered on these pages will help you in many ways. You'll be able to judge this by how you handle each interview. Remember, it's **just another step**. Your goal is moving the process forward.

Step seven – make the sale & you get hired

In terms of achieving your initial JSO, getting an offer to work at a job you've been pursuing, seals the deal. The offer you get should fit your JSO nicely. After all, you made the decision to pursue jobs that aligned with your JSO. What's more, at this stage (post interview), you should know the particulars of the job including: starting pay, benefits, hours, location, etc. In other words, by the time you get to Step Seven, there should be few if any surprises when you're finally offered the position.

Keep in mind each job you get is a mile marker accomplishment and not a "stand-alone" event. Early in the seven-step process you should know enough about each potential job to determine if it fits your specific JSO. If it does, continue going after it. If it doesn't, let it go.

This same consideration should be applied to Step Seven job offers you receive. For example, say you learn something about a job after being interviewed that indicates the position doesn't really align with your JSO. What to do? In most cases, seriously consider dropping out of the running. If the differences between your JSO and the details of the job are minor, ask more questions before accepting. I know this can be hard, but I also know that accepting an offer that's off the mark for you can be devastating.

If you work diligently using the approach presented here in *Get Beyond Your Troubled Past*, the job offers you receive will be congruent with your Plan. Put your faith in this approach and do what needs to be done.

Delivering The Mail

You must be the master of your own narrative, after all it's your story. But you're not a fiction writer or a spin doctor. Making things up or skewing the facts to suit a more palatable version of reality isn't part of the plan and counter to everything presented in this book.

Your narrative is the condensed version of your story. You'll use it to construct the message, or "Mail" you need to deliver. In the world of public relations, this is called managing your message. That perspective fits perfectly in this situation. You already know there are things about you and parts of your story that place you at a competitive disadvantage to others trying to sell their services to the same buyers. Delivering The Mail, or DTM, is designed to help you compete by managing the message so it doesn't manage you.

Here's another tip. When you're introducing yourself, following up, or interviewing, you never really know who you're talking to in the moment. Sure, you may know the person's position and title. You might know what they do and where they do it. But you probably don't know their motivations or their professional or personal agendas. We all have them. You also don't know about any background issues they or others close to them might possess. You just don't know. Therefore, keep the delivery and content of your "Mail" tight and consistent. If you change up and wing it with each delivery, there's no way for you to compare and measure different responses you get from different people. The value of a practiced, thoughtfully constructed message will become obvious once you begin making deliveries. Here's how to do it.

Pull it all together

In Chapter Seven I asked you to write out your Narrative. You'll use it now to create a three or four sentence statement conveying only **the outcome** of your story. Your DTM and your story are **not the same**. The delivery of the full version of your Narrative might come later, but never in the beginning. **I repeat, never.**

If you haven't done so already, start by writing your Narrative as I instructed in Chapter Seven. Next, review your finished version, highlighting four sentences describing how things turned out. The subject of your DTM is what an employer will discover anyway when and if they hire you. Take these four sentences and create your DTM statement. Keep it to four sentences or less.

Practice delivering your mail

Does practice make perfect? We're not after perfection. Instead, your goal is developing a smooth, concise delivery. Just as actors do, you must do as well. Yet there's another critical element that applies directly to you and your situation. It's about the impact of your emotions. Practice gets your delivery down and moves excess emotion out of the way. Your emotions will never completely vanish; however, with practice you'll learn to manage them within you, which in turn will lessen the impact they'll have on others.

Seek and deliver at the best time

Your mission is identifying the first available, yet appropriate, time to DTM. Don't lead with it, but don't hold back looking for the absolute perfect moment, either. Instead, listen and stay heads up. Look for clues, such as references to work history gaps or pauses at certain points in the conversation. When spotted, go ahead and interject. You can start your three or four sentence Delivering The Mail statement by saying something like, *"Well, Mr. Johnson, I'm glad you brought that up, you see I'm ...,"* and proceed with your DTM. As you gain experience doing this, the value of getting to it early will become clear. By delivering early, you have an opportunity to influence the course of events because you're framing the discussion. Waiting means someone else selects the time of delivery. You don't want this, so seek the first appropriate opportunity, and let your DTM roll with precision and low-key candor.

Strike the right tone

The points above are about *what* and *when*. This point is about *how*. Endeavor to strike a balance between coming on too strong or too light. This is a very important step, so be careful not to "cloud-up" or get shaky during your delivery. Conversely, avoid an overly casual approach that will cause the other person to wonder, *"Why?"* given the seriousness of the situation. Practice alone in front of a mirror and then with trusted friends and family. Never forget, it's not what you intend to say that counts; it's how the other person receives it that matters.

Build rapport and relating

Remember, **you're looking for a person and not a job**. Your delivery will help you do this. You are sharing the condensed version of your story because it must be done. You also share because you want to be the person making the delivery in order to control the message. But your delivery also gives you an opportunity to see how others handle your DTM. Watch closely in a relaxed way, something that will come with practice. As you deliver, do they

- Show interest?

- Ask questions?

- Lean forward or back while listening?

- Offer additional information about themselves or others when receiving your DTM?

You're on a mission and must proceed ahead regardless of the outcome. Yet, don't overlook how the other person responds. They'll give you clues and some of these may be important rapport-building tip-offs. Stay heads-up and alert as they receive your DTM.

In spite of the need to deliver and the seriousness of the subject, remind yourself your approach is sales based. People only buy from people they like. So, whose business is it to be likable? It's your business. If you're not likeable, you're not hire-able. So remain in alignment and be authentic as you deliver. This is accomplished with practice. Your goal is to be pleasant and businesslike, which translates as likeability.

Share your DTM and move on

See your DTM as a separate mini-mission, something you do as part of your overall approach. Do it as best you can and move on. The delivery is made in real time; once it's done, it's done. Debrief yourself but don't dwell on or stew over it. Stay on task by remaining fully present. Then, move forward giving your full attention to whatever comes next in the process.

The Wrap-up

A lot goes into achieving your JSO using my approach. I'm aware of this. Yet, I still haven't included everything. Part of this has to do with the overall length of the book but it's also because I don't want to water down the core message.

Take being and staying organized, for example. This is critical for you. I will show you how to keep track of the contacts you make in Chapter Eleven. However, and I'll be frank here, in advance of the upcoming discussion, if you aren't naturally organized, suck it up and seek help immediately. Your way of doing things may place you at a disadvantage in securing your initial position, not to mention accomplishing everything you must do in preparation to reach this stage.

It's very important to keep track of where you go, who you meet, the applications you complete, and the follow-ups you make—all of it. If you can set it up, that's great. If you can't, admit it and go out and find the right person to help you. We all know someone with the abilities we don't possess.

Your initial job is discussed in detail in Chapter Nine. Make no mistake, achieving your JSO and succeeding at your first job is a Really Big Deal. The overall goal is to have positive and significant experience, one that propels you like your own personal tsunami wave, far into the future. I'm looking forward to explaining how this can all come about.

Action Steps

Use your narrative and create your DTM statement.

Practice communicating your DTM statement so it flows effortlessly.

Do this live with family and friends as if rehearsing for a stage presentation.

Chapter Nine

Retaining Your First Job

As you begin your initial "foot-in-the-door" position, keep in mind that you're there on purpose. You didn't grab the first job that came along, and you didn't take any old job just because you were tired of looking. Securing and working at this job is an integral part of your plan. You're there because reaching long-term goals requires attaining short-term objectives, which you've done by landing your initial position.

Your focus now shifts from job search to job retention. This means, you're going to place emphasis on keeping your first job versus excelling at it. You might feel I'm setting the bar too low. If so, reel it in. This stage is all about keeping your job and rebuilding your work history. There will be plenty of opportunities to stand out each day by supplying your employer with solid service, so concentrate on first things first.

This chapter breaks down your time with this first employer into four parts, examining each from the standpoint of retention and progression.

- Your first 120 days, months one through four

- Confirming the deal, months five through eight

- Spreading your wings, months nine through twelve

- Looking around, months thirteen through eighteen

First, we'll look at the perspective I'd like you to adopt while working in this important first position, then we'll discuss the four parts listed above.

Personal Perspective

Success on your initial job depends on you and the perspective you bring to work each day. Remind yourself from day one that you're a Free Agent, and you've entered into an agreement with your new employer to provide service in return for a paycheck. Think of yourself as being like a window cleaning service or a heating and air conditioning contractor, a provider of a service. Although your job classification is that of "employee," consider this as only a category. What you're actually providing your employer with is a product in the form of your service. You choose to continue selling this product to this same customer until it's time to find a new one.

A big factor in your success will be your ability to see yourself this way. However, don't expect everyone else to share this perspective. You'll encounter co-workers who have a very different take on working and being an employee, one not based on being a provider of a service. Don't be influenced by their attitude or way of thinking. Chances are, the only thing you have in common is you all work for the same employer. How they got there and why they remain isn't your concern. Just know you're there on purpose because you took proactive steps to get there. Plus, being there serves a specific purpose for you—to meet short-range objectives leading to long-term goals.

I'll level with you, you've got a lot riding on this first job. It's not because you're incapable of finding another, or because you should feel grateful in some negative, reactive way. Not at all. It's because it took a lot to get to this point and starting again from scratch would be especially tough considering your background. Imagine yourself like an old-fashioned traveling circus having to take down all the concessions and tents, load up the train, travel to the next spot, unload, set up, and begin the show all over again. If it doesn't work out with your first job this is exactly what happens.

The time line

Before looking at how Walter did on his first job and discussing the four stages of your initial job, let's review how this period fits within the context of your Five-year Plan. From the time you develop your plan and initial JSO until the beginning of your first job, weeks or months will have passed. Let's assume it took six months just to make things easy to calculate, even though it could take less time. If you work for eighteen months at your first job, you'll be at the two-year mile marker by the time you move on to your second employer.

Of course, these are estimates and your situation may be a little different. But think and plan your intermediate objectives based on this timeline. There are benefits to you personally, and as an employee, in planning your exit strategy even before you start your first job. It serves as a reminder that you have a plan and you're working toward achieving the goals contained within your plan. It also helps you stay engaged as someone providing a service **on purpose** which will help you avoid the temptation to "settle in."

Walter's Steady, Sure Approach

Walter looked tired as he cleared the top step. A large full plastic bag hung from his left hand. He glanced toward my office, and I waved him to come over.

"Walter you look beat. Is everything okay?" I asked as he positioned the bag on the floor and sat down.

"I'm tired ... what is it, almost five o' clock?" He leaned forward to see the clock above my desk. "Wow, 5:20, I've been out all day looking for clothes. I went to three thrift stores. Took the whole day with all the bus transfers I had to make." Walter reached for the bag pulling out two sports jackets, three shirts, a pair of brown dress shoes, a belt, and a whole pile of socks. "I received my first check yesterday which wasn't much, but at least I could get all this stuff."

Walter was into his third week as a sales representative at one of the art galleries in the Miracle Mile Shops at Planet Hollywood. He was paid minimum wage plus commission, but he started mid-pay period and only made a few small sales. He filled me in a couple of days ago before leaving for work.

"So are things dropping into place at the gallery?" I watched Walter methodically fold each garment before placing it back in the bag.

"I hope I make the cut. I think I'm doing okay but it's hard to tell. It's a little cut-throat. Anyway, we'll see. I have my one-month review coming up at the end of next week. One thing is for sure; I have to get my wardrobe up to speed. What I've been wearing is pretty sad compared to some of the other sales associates. But these should help." He gestured to the neatly packed bag.

Walter didn't need much assistance when it came to understanding the importance of alignment and looking the part. He'd done it for years in his former life but, as an inmate on work-release, he didn't have much to work with. He'd managed to assemble a reasonable set of clothes to land the job but it was tough washing and ironing the few items he had over and over to maintain his work schedule.

"You still like it? I asked. "The other day when we talked you seemed fired up to head out and get to work." And he did. He was leaving a little after noon, working a 2:00 to 10:30 pm shift. He was pumped to get moving.

"Oh yes, absolutely, I like working there and the customers are all over the map, really. You never know who'll walk in. I think I can make decent money once I get a little more time under my belt." Walter stroked his small, gray mustache and looked out the window, taking in the view for a few beats. He straightened and repositioned himself in his chair, hunching his shoulders and rolling his head down a little and to the left, a small twitch of sorts I'd seen many times from him. "Right now I'm concentrating on making it past this review because I think that's all they do. You either fit in or you don't. If you can't sell, they'll cut you loose after a couple months. I'm not worried about that, it's about being consistent and working my way into the rotation. The sales will come. This is a good gig for me right now."

That's exactly what he did. His evaluation was cursory at best. Walter progressively built his sales week by week. He was "in." So he kept going to work, dressing better as the weeks went by and his paychecks continued to climb. Walter planned to get back to the life he had before going to prison. To do this, he needed to maintain the gallery job for a while after being released. He was disciplined and motivated. He understood his situation; he was a Free Agent, able to compete in the Marketplace once again.

Your Initial Job in Four Parts

Your first 120 days: months one through four

Starting a new job is both exciting and stressful. You're learning a lot, being challenged, and generally coming up to speed. It's also when most employees have to navigate a sixty- or ninety-day probationary period, where they're judged and graded on punctuality, ability to do the work, and overall "fit" with the business or organization.

An evaluation period comes as no surprise, so most people make an effort to put their best foot forward during this phase. I assume you will, too. But take a moment to consider the following questions. Will you

1. Try hard just because you're being scored?

2. Or, do it anyway even if you weren't being judged?

Giving your best, **only** because you're under the microscope isn't good enough. It's reactive. Make it your business to do well because **it's your business**. You're in the "providing a service" business. Your perspective should be that this evaluation period will determine if you'll continue doing business with this particular customer.

Confirming the deal: months five through eight

Once the dew is off the rose and your probationary period passes, work usually becomes a bit more routine. This is where you have the opportunity to "seal the deal" by showing your employer that your solid performance during the first few months wasn't a fluke. The way you make this happen is by *showing through doing* and by supplying a great service.

However, when you get to this stage, you enter **a honeymoon danger zone** that's taken down more than a few people in your shoes. You may not see it or realize it, but this Marketplace booby trap of sorts can vacuum you up in a heartbeat. Let me explain.

By your fifth month, the spotlight no longer shines on you quite as brightly. Things that were new and uncommon at first have become familiar. Your quest to find the job has seen victory, and you've made it over the probationary hump. You're now a staff member. Benefits will soon start kicking in and you may have received a pat on the back.

If you're reacting and not piloting your own "service boat," it's natural to be tempted into easing up a little at this point. "After all," you may reason, "I passed the test, and I'm now in. Besides, others didn't make it this far. Hey, they're already talking about bumping me up!"

Well, this is no time to drop your guard or take your eye off the ball. Avoid this by staying heads-up and focused on exactly **why** you're there.

The part about possibly getting "bumped up" introduces an important point. In businesses where turnover and duty pile-on are high, it's become common for employees barely past probation to get promoted to lower level supervisory roles. This could happen in spite of your background snag because you're doing a great job. If it does, stay wide awake and proceed with extreme caution for two reasons:

- First, a fast move up may be an indication of a pressed and stressed management team; not directly tied to your skills and abilities.

- Second, you may not be ready for the pressure an entry-level lead position can bring.

Remember that you're there to provide a good service and work your plan. Think carefully before accepting this type of "reward" because it can knock you off track and lock you into duties that don't align with your original JSO and master plan. You're in charge of your own future. Be wary of any early promotion if it solves a problem that belongs to someone else.

Spreading your wings: months nine through twelve

It's time for a short review. You began with a plan and your JSO, which you achieved. You passed through the probationary period and confirmed during the last four months picking you was the right decision. Now, you can spread your wings and show what else you have to offer. This is where you dig a little deeper and reach a little higher as a worker who provides an excellent service. While doing this, take note and do the following:

- Stay engaged without getting caught up in politics and drama

- Make a Discovery List of what comes easily and naturally, and what doesn't

- Lay the groundwork for meeting people and positioning

Your discovery list

During the last eight months, you've learned a few new things about yourself as a worker and as a person. For example, something you thought would be difficult turned out to be easy. Or, something you thought you were great at doing wasn't quite so easy.

Good, you have items for your Discovery List. This is a list or journal of what you've learned and discovered while employed at your first job. You've been on the job long enough to take stock, so look back and start making notes. Add to it regularly, paying special attention to skills and procedures you learn. Don't overlook work-related experiences and situations that require a little extra navigation on your part. These are usually related to soft skills you've developed. This information will come in handy as you begin meeting new people and positioning yourself for a move to your next employer.

Meeting people and positioning

As I watched prison inmates struggle to find work-release employment, it drove home just how difficult it can be for background-burdened people to gain an employment toehold, especially in the digital age. Plus, just getting a job wasn't enough because, as ex-offenders, most were starting out in entry-level positions.

The goal beyond finding a job is keeping it, so you can eventually become self-sufficient. But most entry-level jobs are low wage. To have a shot at self-sufficiency, you have to move up with your current employer. Or, more than likely, you'll move away to another employer offering higher pay and possibly better benefits, too.

The inmates I watched needed to meet people and network, a difficult task given their re-entry, work-release status. You'll need to meet people and network, too. Thankfully, it'll be easier for you than it was for them.

This re-entry example points to a problem shared by many background-challenged people, a lack of experience developing and retaining business relationships. The term "networking" covers a lot of ground. To simply say you need to get out and start networking is too vague. So let's narrow it down to what I call "Positioning Through Relationships" or PTR.

PTR refers to deliberately meeting and developing relationships with people to position you toward accomplishing your five-year, career-based plan. This may sound pretty self-centered and "all about me" but, to be truly effective, it can't remain that way. Networking speaks of the need to find and connect with people so you overcome the built-in limitations of background snags. After all, as you know by now you aren't looking for a job, you're looking for a person.

This is exactly what successful business people do continuously, they meet new people, developing connections and relationships that lead to the achievement of their business objectives. Let's not forget, you're a businessperson too. You're an independent seller of your services in the Marketplace, and you'll continue selling these services as long as you remain in the workforce. After you pass the one-year point with your first "foot-in-the-door" job, it's time to develop your PTR strategy for your move on to your next employer.

Avoiding politics and drama

Always be mindful as a person with a background problem; you have more at stake on the job than those without background issues. Starting another job search from scratch at this point would be a major setback. Doing the job is one thing, playing your cards right when it comes to everything else happening at work, is another. My advice is always keep things tight and business-like. Remain "on edge" and "on purpose."

You've made it this far and accomplished numerous things, but your background may make you still feel like an outsider. Regardless of our differences, most of us share the need to belong and feel accepted. In spite of Hollywood's image of the independent man or woman taking on the world, our social evolution draws us toward groups. Studies show about eighty percent of the population see themselves as "belongers." Don't be surprised if you start feeling good about being part of something. If so, bring this feeling to the surface and air it out. Be careful. You're not there "to join in," you're there to provide a service.

I don't want you to feel as though you're isolated or you don't belong. Yet wanting to belong, be included, and experience the warm fuzzies of being part of an inner circle, can bring on problems. You're there to work and build a few business relationships, not find life-long friendships. This is a real danger zone especially if you've been out of the Marketplace for a while.

174

Or, if you've forgotten how nice it feels to be back on track. Examine your desire to belong. Stay alert and aware when others try to draw you in, because they will.

The antidote for this is to stay on the edge. Work hard, do a great job, and get to know people. But steer clear of the complications that often come with belonging. To state it bluntly, it's **way too early** to add complexity to your life. Your mission is too important to risk getting caught up in the inevitable company politics and drama. As a newly hired employee, it's easy to miss this point.

You've worked hard to find the job, secure it, and now keep it. All the other stuff that comes with working remains largely unexamined. It's stuff you didn't create. Don't set yourself up for getting sideswiped. Be aware of the formal and informal activities around you. Keep in mind every day why you're there and remember to stay "**on edge**" and "**on purpose**."

Looking around: months thirteen through eighteen

While you continue doing a stellar job back at the ranch, the time has come to prepare to make your move to another employer. As you gear up to start looking, here are a few things I'd like you to do.

Create a new Job Search Objective

Simply take your first one and update it. Don't dwell on it, stew, or sweat it—just bring your thoughts together and focus on your next logical step.

Update your résumé

Add your current employer and position to your résumé. Update your JSO and make whatever small adjustments are necessary based on your growing Discovery List. Don't burden yourself with this, you're updating and tweaking only. Nothing more is needed.

Get business cards

Keep them simple and inexpensive. Include your name, phone number, email address, and a brief statement about what you do. For the statement, be concise and perhaps clever, but avoid cutesy. Cutesy doesn't fly well in business. Keep it to just one sentence. Considering the range in quality from good to poor I see on the web and in print, I hesitate to say this; however, pictures known as head shots, have become common on business cards, so you may want to include one. If so, it must be appropriate, business-like, and a quality image; otherwise, skip the photo. Print the cards on the front only, leaving the back blank. Don't use glossy paper. You want people to write notes on the back of your card. Make it easy. The bottom line on business cards is this— keep them clean, crisp, simple, and up to date. I suggest sticking with white or ivory paper.

Tell your current employer

There are two sides of the coin regarding whether or not to inform your employer. I advocate sharing this information, but be cool about it. You've been honest and truthful with them about your background, so continue in this vein regarding your long-term aspirations. Make sure you clearly communicate this doesn't involve anything immediate. You want to be able to move freely, taking a look at future employment options without feeling like you're sneaking behind your employer's back, so tell them. Look for ways to draw them in and keep them posted on what you see while you're out and about. Do this right and your supervisor may start asking what you've uncovered, because he might be looking as well.

Telling your employer you won't be around forever can be a tough task. The good news is that you won't be doing it for a while, so you'll have plenty of time to wrap your head around the idea. Look, this is business. That's an inescapable fact. There's nothing guaranteed with your first or any other employer.

Occasionally, a person lands the perfect job and it's an ideal fit right out of the gate. But that's incredibly rare. So, as a practical matter, once you pass the one-year point, **plan** for the need to move on to another position which takes you to the next mile marker on your journey toward success. Know going in that you plan to exit. Plant the seeds about your intentions as you establish yourself. The tenth month is a good time to deliver the news on this before you actually start going out. Be mindful how you do it and, no matter what, don't stop dishing out a top-notch service while kicking the tires in preparation for your next job.

This job search will be different from your first one. Here's an example to give you an idea based on my extensive experience assisting background-challenged job seekers in the culinary field. The essence of this approach can be applied to any field. I'll expand on this in greater detail in the PTR discussion in Chapter Ten.

Example – moving to your second job

Insert yourself into this example. Regardless of your field of employment or your own JSO, pretend you're the person I'm describing. Mentally walk yourself through each step, bringing all your senses to bear. See the place, hear the sounds, and smell the aromas.

Let's say your Five-year Goal is to become a sous chef with one of the major restaurants on the legendary Las Vegas Strip. Your initial JSO was to find a prep-cook position with a franchise restaurant. You accomplished this by getting hired by a regional chain, Sandy's Diner. You've been with Sandy's on Tropicana Road just over ten months and things are going well. Your manager gave you a shot, and he's turned out to be a decent, fair guy. That's good but also bad, because staff turnover is near zero. The situation is crystal clear—there's little room for advancement.

So, it's time to start looking around. You made a point of mentioning this to your manager, by dropping hints and seeds at first, followed by out and out telling him your intentions. Your message is you're serious about moving up in the culinary field. The time has come to see what's out there. Plus, you kid around with him about becoming a manager just like him at the new Sandy's being built across town. He's fine with all this because he gets it and offers to be a good reference for you when the time comes. In the meantime, you continue working hard and enjoying your job.

Your plan is to move from Sandy's in about six months. First, you list the businesses that match your new JSO. Select from the list and plot out as many physical visits as you can manage during the next few months. You want to check out their location, facility, menu, service, and meet the manager. Who knows, you may even get a chance to see a few kitchens.

Pick one or two places to visit each week. This example requires you to play the role of a customer. Actually, you'll be a paying customer, ordering something inexpensive to keep your costs down. The idea is to experience the place from a patron's perspective, not a job seeker's perspective. Just as you're finishing whatever you ordered, ask to speak to the manager. The server will ask if everything is okay. You reply in a straightforward and pleasant way that everything's fine, but you'd like to speak to the manager. The server wonders, "What the ...," but of course gets the manager.

Soon the manager appears saying something like, "Hi, I'm Rebecca the House Manager, can I help you?"

You stand, smile, and introduce yourself. "Hi, Rebecca, my name is John, and I'm cooking at Sandy's on Tropicana Road. I wanted to introduce myself. The grilled chicken sandwich was great by the way." You hand her your card. Be prepared for a quick conversation if the opportunity develops.

However it ends, thank her and say, "I'm happy at Sandy's for the time being but 'you never know.'" That's all you say about searching for a new job unless she probes. You've planted a seed and can connect back with her later.

That's how it works. Your intention is to keep it short and sweet. If she gives you more time to talk or offers to take you on a short tour of the back of the house, great. But keep your social antenna up and active. If the place is busy, don't press it. The manager will notice that you noticed. This is **targeted networking** in action.

You leave with her name, card, and whatever else she was willing to share and provide to you. Your updated résumé was with you, but you **didn't** mention it or use it because the purpose of your visit wasn't distributing résumés or talking about job opportunities. If she asks, of course you would've been prepared to give it to her. But your real goal was educating and introducing yourself.

Do this with many businesses matching your new JSO. Educate yourself and meet people in this specific, targeted way. It's important to keep track of every trip you make and each person you meet. I recommend sending a brief email after each visit, thanking them and telling them you'll stay in touch. By making these trips and introductions, you're building a list you'll use as you get closer to an actual job search. I'll expand on the best ways to use your growing list and get the search for your second position underway in Chapter Ten.

The Wrap-up

What does job retention mean? Simply put it means doing your job well in order to keep your job, until it's time to find another. Things will change for you once you begin working. The energy you expended just to find and lock-in your position will now become redirected to actually doing the job. The factors contributing to this are

- The dynamics of the business

- The behavior of others working around you

- The demands of your job duties

All these become like magnets drawing you toward the center of the organization and away from your goals and objectives. You must be aware of this inward pull while staying awake to the importance of providing the best service you can, even if the person next to you is whining, playing victim, and cutting corners. You have a big goal and it's important to remain locked on achieving it. Let your plan and your personal mission to provide a great service be your guides propelling you through each day of work at this crucial first job.

In Chapter Ten, we'll examine Positioning Through Relationships or PTR in detail. This is essential as you advance toward all your remaining mile markers.

Action Steps

Maintain a journal or log and from it develop your Discovery List.

Prepare for your next job, taking specific note of the material in this chapter listed under Looking Around: Months Thirteen through Eighteen.

Chapter Ten

Positioning Yourself

for JSO Success

Chapters Seven, Eight, and Nine were about finding, securing, and retaining your first job. You were introduced to the idea of positioning using the example of seeking a job at a restaurant similar to Michael's situation. In Chapter Ten, we'll expand on the discussion about positioning, and we'll also tackle what is a difficult situation for some, actually leaving their first job. As we dive in, keep in mind the "twin guides" that influence your decisions, your plan and your personal mission to supply a great service.

Why Position Yourself?

Let's say you don't want to leave your first job. Generally, this situation falls into one of three categories.

- You like it and that's what matters. If so, you're probably wearing blinders.

- You see some benefit to being there regardless of liking or not liking it. However, if you don't like it, that benefit won't last.

- You're avoiding the search for job number two. Seriously?

Staying put

For the moment forget you went into this first job with a plan. You're there now, you like it, and you want to stay. If it works out, fantastic. Really, I mean it because your overall goal is finding satisfaction and success in whatever field you pursue. However, as noted in the last chapter, the odds of finding a perfect fit with your first job are slight. When I say "a perfect fit" I mean one which provides you with

- The financial return you'll need

- Opportunity for advancement and growth

- An environment and situation you'll continue enjoying

As a practical matter, there's no way to determine any of this until you've been on the job awhile. Consequently, any thought of staying before you've been there at least one year is probably irrelevant. When you reach the one-year mark, haul out the three criteria points above and do your own assessment. If you have solid guarantees in each category, fine. However, I'm willing to bet this won't be the case. So, how could positioning yourself **not be** in your best interest?

I seriously doubt you'll have the assurances you need to stay. Plus, I believe **nearly everyone** needs to position themselves and **absolutely everyone** can benefit from positioning. Furthermore, knowing what else is out there and connecting with other people in your field makes you a better employee.

Proceed ahead

In the last chapter, I introduced you to the concept of positioning and Positioning Through Relationships (PTR). Here's my definition of positioning in the context of achieving your Five-year Goal.

Positioning is everything you do to enhance the likelihood of gaining success, according to plan, at each stage of the process. Positioning places a high value on select interpersonal relationships, and it includes things you do and don't do to develop and enhance those relationships. It determines, among other things, who you'll meet, which groups you'll join, and what certification courses you'll enroll in.

Your positioning steps actually begin as soon as your Five-year Goal and Plan are in place and written down. However, it isn't until several months after you start your initial job, that positioning really kicks in as a direct action step. Prior to this, you've concentrated on securing and succeeding at your foot-in-the-door job. View everything that went into finding and succeeding at your job as one big positioning act. Why? It creates a platform upon which the rest of your positioning work will be built if you do it right.

Although you may not realize it at first, positioning will come to play a big role in your success. Every step you take is a positioning step and is laid out by design in a methodical, purposeful manner. If compared to an athletic playbook, it details how you plan to win The Big Game—how you prepare, create a game plan, and strategize each move leading to minute-by-minute implementation of the plan.

Think of positioning in terms of set-ups and plays. Your preparation and strategy got you in the game with your first job. Your ongoing conditioning and practice will ensure your success as you play the game and work at your job. Now it's time to survey the field, gauging the tempo and flow of the game.

When you consider your positioning moves, keep one eye on the big picture, your Master Plan. Keep the other eye on your JSO. Be creative yet simple in your solutions to the questions below. Many people make this way too complicated. Avoid complexity and simply ask yourself

- What move will I make next?

- Why am I making this move?

- Who are the players in the game?

- How are my moves and the players linked to my ultimate goal?

Continuing with the role you played in the restaurant scenario provided in Chapter Nine, here's an example of how you could answer the questions:

Q) What move will I make next?

A) To discover for myself, by physically visiting restaurants that meet my criteria, what options are available to me.

Q) Why am I making it?

A) I intend to leave Sandy's within the next six to eight months, so I need to visit other places and build a list of possible contacts.

Q) Who are the players?

A) Me of course, my current manager, and all the new restaurant contacts I develop while out and about.

Q) How will my moves and the players involved link to my ultimate goal?

A) Getting out educates me and puts me face to face with people who can hire me. It will also link me to others who can hire me for my next job. This advances me toward the next mile marker on my path leading directly to my long-term goal.

Consider what this positioning example leaves out. It's not general business networking. I'm referring to attending open or general networking functions where people from various business fields come together, connect, and exchange business cards with the purpose of developing leads. In the example from Chapter Nine, if there was a local restaurant industry expo, conference, or food service gathering of some kind, it would be appropriate to attend. But general networking is exactly that, general in scope. The potential return is too small to justify the time and effort.

By comparison, going out and visiting pre-selected establishments has a far higher potential Return on Investment (ROI). Your ROI can increase even more by

- How your contacts are made

- The techniques you use working with people

- The quality and effectiveness of your follow-up activities

- The relationships you develop with people through follow-up

Links in the Chain

In Chapter Nine, I introduced the concept of Positioning Through Relationships or PTR, which was defined as deliberately meeting and developing connections with people to position yourself to accomplish your career-based plan. Think of each relationship as a link in a chain. Your task is building links, something shared by most networking activities. But here's the deal, when it comes to your PTR, never break a link once it's established. Never.

Imagine this chain is the primary support connecting you to your Five-year Plan and Goal. Picture the chain supporting a narrow bridge suspended across a deep gorge. The starting point of your career journey is on one side. Your big goal sits on the opposite side. You must traverse the gorge using the bridge to reach your goal, all the while paying close attention to the condition of the chain because even one broken link will cause the entire bridge to fall into the gorge.

Let's assume you hold all the power when it comes to maintaining these relationships. Certainly, strong relationships between two people require effort from both. But, for our people-link relationship example, let's give you all the marbles. This means it's your responsibility to build the links and keep them strong. Why? You're the one proactively constructing the bridge to get to your goal on the other side. Therefore, the task of maintaining the chain which holds up the bridge leading to your goal **should be your responsibility**.

Back to the links. Remember, each link represents a person. Imagine the same mental chain and bridge over the gorge. In your mind replace the links with people, picture them locking their arms together like a chain, from one side to the other. These are your "people-links" who'll assist you in getting across the imaginary gorge to your next job. Your positioning mission is selecting people-links who'll make this happen.

Next, let's ante-up the pot. Picking people-links at random won't work. Random links are too weak and, besides, there's no assurance the other person is capable to actually being a link in your chain. Instead select strong people-links, willing to help hold up your bridge with you. Therefore, pick and choose carefully.

Once you add a new people-link to your chain, it's your duty to see they remain solid and well maintained. If a crack develops, it's up to you to repair it so it's strong again.

Now you've built your bridge supported by people-links. Why not toss in another condition? Your people-links must be arranged in a specific order. Slapping them together any old which way will cause your chain to corrode and eventually fail. As a responsible bridge owner, you need to pay close attention to **the location of each link**.

This is how I want you to see your own PTR, as building a chain composed of carefully, hand-picked links, arranged in order, to support your bridge which gets you to your goal.

In the restaurant example, you discovered how to search for potential people-links. You'll do something similar and, in the process, meet many people, some of which will become contacts. From contacts come people-links. Your primary task is to narrow the field to find these few critical people-links.

Link building is relationship building

Building relationship links is truly a proactive task. As discussed in Chapter Four, many background-challenged people unfortunately default to reactive behaviors. Perhaps this is one reason why link building for positioning doesn't always come easy. Also, many personal and work-related links may have been shattered in the past due to events leading up to the background problem. The point is that PTR activities, in general, and link building, in particular, may require effort to develop.

But link building doesn't have to be difficult. It's based on the introduction process I covered in Chapter Eight, a task you'll be accustomed to by the time your PTR begins in earnest. Communication and alignment also come into play. As you meet people while searching for possible people-links, concentrate on how other people receive your message. Part of your overall "messaging" is your alignment, which means you and your objective must fit together tightly. This is crucial because you'll tell the potential link-person what you aim to achieve. Everything must seem congruent and make sense to the other person; otherwise, they won't get it and won't want to help.

The most meaningful link-building tool is the platform you'll develop by producing a great service to your first employer. This experience will bolster your confidence and provide reference points to determine your second JSO. Don't forget your Discovery List and field notes taken during your first job. They should contain all sorts of goodies and nuggets you can utilize when interviewing potential people-links.

You will discover just how valuable people-links can be when it comes to pursuing your second job. Your first job experience will produce two important things that you will continue to build upon as you advance toward your ultimate goal. The first is a positive work experience. The second is job references. Again, returning to one of the crucial concepts of my job search approach, you're looking for a person, not a job. Why? Because people, not paper or digits, will help you traverse and rise above the barriers caused by your background issues.

As you prepare for your move to job number two, one of your primary tasks will be to connect the people-links at your first job with those links you will make in connection to your second job. Picture yourself working in your own personal "Link and Chain Workshop," earnestly and thoughtfully joining links together. In practical terms, this begins when your new people-links check your references, most likely made up of people-links developed during your first job. I want you to see this for what it is— something you orchestrated and set in motion.

Now imagine yourself back at the point when life was the darkest. The last thing on earth you wanted was anything remotely associated with people linking up and putting two plus two together. No way. There were too many issues and too many complications involved. It seemed better to lay low and react. By the time you get deep into positioning yourself, you'll have come a long way from those days.

Roger Gets his Groove Back

I was happily surprised when Roger not only made our Tuesday appointment but also completed the assignments I gave him. There was no outward appearance of his stumble less than a week earlier. In fact, he looked nice, wearing gray dress slacks, a button down black shirt, well-polished black shoes, and a fresh shave. As I watched him settle his tall frame into the chair, it hit me. Roger reminded me of actor, Bruce Dern. Even his hair, graying and tousled, brought the actor to mind.

"You look good Roger. It's nice to see you," I paused, "I wasn't sure you'd return ...."

Roger took in a deep breath. "No, John, I planned to come back all along. I realize it didn't look like it after my little episode at O'Reilly's, but what you said about where I'm going and what I want made sense." He placed the completed papers on my desk. "I can't do that anymore. So, call it one last fling? I don't know. Anyway, my words aren't worth much right now. It's time to get busy doing something." He sat back, crossed his arms, and gave himself a big bear hug. "I found an apartment yesterday. I'm moving in this weekend." Roger nodded his head as if confirming to himself he'd made the right move.

"I have to ask. Was it because of the episode? Did your sister ask you to move out?"

"No, it was my decision. She's been good to me. Her husband Freddie's been good too. It was time. They're doing better now and don't need financial help from me like they did before ...." He took another deep breath, exhaling in one big burst. "For heaven's sake, John, I'm going on 45 years old. Enough of this crap. I gotta get moving."

We spent the rest of our time reviewing his Five-year Plan and JSO. Roger wanted to remain in Las Vegas, eventually buying a home in the Green Valley area, an upscale suburb. He wanted to pursue a career in the wholesale painting supply business. The housing market was showing signs of life again, and he felt it was a good time to get in.

Roger was skilled on the computer and his résumé was done before our fourth meeting. There was no old business to clean up and he was ready to get out and introduce himself. Here's the fascinating part, he found a job before our fourth meeting, too. I almost fell out of my chair when I listened to his phone message.

"Hey John, it's Roger. You won't believe it, but I got a job at Morgen's Paint Supply working as an in-house wholesale associate. I can't believe it man. They were only the third place I visited. Third time's the charm, I guess. I just went in and introduced myself the way we discussed. Next thing I knew, I'm in the back talking with the owner. He seemed interested, but you know how that goes. Anyway, he made a couple of calls and got back to me this morning. I'm doing the drug test tomorrow. My start date is next Monday. Wow!"

As it turned out, his meeting with the owner was a condensed session including introduction, Q&A, and Delivering The Mail, all rolled into one. As you know, I don't recommend accelerating the process, especially when it comes to an early "mail delivery." But the owner turned out to be a recovering alcoholic, sober for many years. Even though he didn't know Roger, he was intuitive, asking direct, probing questions. Roger responded openly and truthfully. The owner liked Roger immediately and the rest, as they say, is history.

I checked in frequently with Roger; after all, there was a lot on his plate when we started. At our first meeting, he appeared "anxious, uncertain, and stuck." That was before having a mini-relapse, moving out of his sister's home, and starting a new job, all in less than two months. But he seemed like he was doing fine with both his recovery and his new job. He told me he liked working at Morgen's and made sure to put out more than was expected every day. There wasn't much in the way of politics or drama from what he said, so keeping things business-like was fairly easy.

Just before Roger's one-year anniversary, I called to talk with him about positioning. Roger told me he didn't need to do it because he decided to stay right there. I suggested we sit down for a little brainstorming session, but he didn't want to hear it. His mind was made up. He was staying. End of story.

I was happy things were going well for Roger, however all his eggs were now in one basket. His choice to skip researching other possibilities concerned me. Even so, Roger, now age 46 was a big boy, and I couldn't make him do anything.

Less than two months later I got a voice mail from Roger.

"John, hey, it's Roger. Sorry I shut you down last time we talked, man. My bad all the way, really. But listen, I'm freakin' out over here. Carl, the owner, sold the business to a supply company out of New Mexico. One minute it's Carl and now we got this dickhead young General Manager messing with everything. This is horrible. No way I can stay here. John, give me a call, I need to talk."

I'll cut to the chase. Roger's now working for a large paint distributor in Las Vegas. He came in a few days after his call, and I helped him update and re-group. The plan was to stay the course at the paint supply job (even though it was in chaos) and to get back out on the introduction circuit while he still worked at Morgen's. Carl, the former owner, was distraught about how everything ended up with the buyout and was more than happy to recommend Roger. Carl turned out to be an exceptional people-link for Roger because of his solid reputation in the painting community.

It took Roger six weeks of heavy lifting and connecting his people-links to nail down the distributor position. Fortunately, he was able to switch his schedule with a co-worker, giving him one day during the week for job searching. During that time, he visited over twenty businesses and had three interviews. His efforts paid off, not only in landing a new job but also in how he got it. By sticking with his updated JSO, Roger built his own contact list. This helped because many of the businesses he visited were customers of the distributor who hired him. Knowing about them, along with Carl's recommendation, eventually did it for Roger.

When the new owner situation at Roger's first job hit the fan, he knew he needed to move fast. Fortunately, he sent the red flag up immediately, wasting little time and getting down to business in short order. Plus, he was contrite, open, and willing to listen. He zeroed in on businesses that matched his new JSO and picked up where he left off prior to being hired by Carl. Here are the pertinent things Roger and I talked about as he mapped out his positioning moves.

Roger's move needed to be

- Aligned - with his master goal, his next mile marker (his next step)

- Involved with people - introductions, meetings, direct contact with people

- Simple, specific, and practical – putting into practice the notion of the shortest distance between two points

- Affordable and achievable - within a limited timeframe

- Calculated and strategic – where one proactive move is worth five reactive ones

- Done the right way - zero points given for "busy work"

Social Media - A Limited Approach

Although Roger didn't need it, there's a case to be made for adding a limited social media presence at this stage. Your second position should build upon the positive work history, service provider mentality, and people-links—all developed while working at your first job. You now have something to show and present to the world which can be used as you gear up for your second job search. This time though, your focus shifts to Positioning Through Relationship or PTR using the platform created by your first job. A small social media presence might assist you in developing new relationship links.

Before entering the social media waters however, ask yourself if you really need it. Roger didn't, neither did the person in the restaurant example. But Roger and our imaginary sous chef might need it in the future to support their **next** JSO, one that will take them up the career ladder.

Consider the social media and internet work you completed from Chapter Six. If you checked and cleared everything and have stayed on the social media sidelines since, it may be time to create a basic presence. If, on the other hand, you didn't complete the clean-up or there were things you couldn't fix, I recommend taking another run at it using a commercial service, if necessary. The point is; don't jump into social media if there's old stuff still floating around. Clean it up first before considering a new approach.

Clearly, if you're pursuing a management or professional job, there's an expectation to have social media exposure on LinkedIn, for example. Yet, you should determine this based on your specific situation. As explained in Chapter Six, **social media comes second** after relationship links. Think carefully about how to do this and don't get ahead of yourself. Success itself doesn't eliminate the background issue. The most effective way to overcome barriers created by background problems is through relationships, which means people-links.

The Wrap-up

The old expression, "It's not what you know, it's who you know," will never disappear. But what if you don't know anyone? Even if you do, what if they aren't the right people? Just finding a job isn't good enough because without people-link relationships, the possibility you'll need to start over again without key relationships to assist you, always exists. Positioning Through Relationships and people-links are concepts I'll refer to and discuss in greater detail in Chapter Eleven.

Action Steps

Plan out the search for your second position using a PTR perspective and mindset.

Review your actual need for a limited social media presence. If you don't need it, don't do it.

Chapter Eleven

Advancing Toward Your Goal

We started the discussion on positioning in Chapter Nine and expanded on it in Chapter Ten. In Chapter Eleven, we'll explore how best to use the information you'll generate as you're meeting people and positioning yourself going forward. The information you gather will be valuable to you in the short term and far into the future. What's more, it belongs to **you**!

Contacts and Links

Keeping track

Before discussing how to keep track of your people-link contacts, let's dig deeper into why positioning through relationships or PTR is essential. As noted, I don't recommend traditional business networking, at least not for the first couple of years working your plan. You need experience first because there's a big difference between talking about what you want to do, and actually doing it. Consequently, your first priority is securing that first job, racking up positive work history, and positioning yourself for your own brand of networking.

After working for a year, you've gained experience, developed contacts, and made a few people-links. That's good but it's a far cry from being ready for mainstream business networking during this time. You're better off concentrating on gaining experience and building your specific contact base than unfocused networking. Your individualized networking will happen in the form of PTR, which is deliberate, targeted, and specific.

Positioning actually starts when you begin searching for your first job. However, I don't recommend setting up and maintaining a formal tracking system then because there are already enough moving parts for you to manage. A good time to start organizing contacts is just before you begin positioning for your second job. Setting up a system at this stage will do two things for you. First, it will reinforce the need to build links by connecting with people. Second, it provides a way to trap and retain all the contact information you'll soon be accumulating.

I can't stress enough how important it is to be single-minded about developing your own targeted contacts. Remember, overcoming background-related barriers requires people in the form of people-links. In most cases, people-links start out as contacts. So, it's of paramount importance to have a way to organize and keep track of all of your contacts.

Here's how to do it for free using a computer or smart phone and the Internet. If you're more of a low-tech person, use index cards and a notebook. Start by setting up two online programs, Insightly and Google Mail (known as Gmail). Both programs are free and, when used together, they will handle all your contact-tracking needs.

If you already have a Google account, sign up for a new one and use it exclusively for positioning activities. Make sure the name you choose is appropriate, yourname@gmail.com is certainly fine, but you may already have it or it might not be available. Whatever you use, keep it business-like and suitable.

Insightly is described as "an integrated online customer relationship management (CRM) and project management" tool. Don't let the name throw you. For you, it's your very own "cloud-based" contact management system accessible from anywhere using your mobile device. You can do a lot with a free account. For example, you can integrate your new Gmail account so emails can be attached to individual contacts.

Insightly is highly intuitive and easy to use. It has a project-management feature that comes in handy for organizing your people-link work and more. But Insightly isn't the only option available; there are other similar products, so research and compare to find one that feels good for you. However, if you want to get right on it, Insightly and Gmail will do the trick.

Regardless of the system you decide on, it's of little value unless you use it. Therefore, don't wait, dig right in, and start getting familiar with it immediately.

You may find setting up your system and learning it are easier to accomplish than inputting the contact information. Entering data isn't difficult but it can be tedious, especially if you let it pile up. To keep this from happening, get in the habit of entering contact information daily.

Keep each contact file up to date by adding notes and attaching emails. Having this information easily available and in one place is vital because the database you create will continue living on and being useful as you progress in your career. Imagine how many category specific contacts (those associated with your JSOs and master goal) you'll have after maintaining your database over several years.

Here's something else to consider. The contact information you accumulate is valuable not only for your PTR and link-building purposes but also for use in helping others in your field. As you move toward your Five-year Goal, you'll come in contact with lots of people. No doubt, some will have background issues like you. These folks will be in the same spot you were in a few years back. They're just starting out and need contacts and people-links. If you stay the course of your plan, it's a virtual certainty you'll become a people-link to others, including people with familiar background issues.

Not all contacts are links

The database you develop should be focused on your field of work. It shouldn't include everyone you know. Put family, friends, and acquaintances on a different list. The majority of entries should be directly tied to your business and career.

Entering and updating information takes time, so let this be a determining factor in whether or not to include a contact. See your database as a helpful tool, but never your master. As you will come to learn, the number of ways you'll use this information will surprise you.

To help you decide how to distinguish between contacts and links consider this: each link you develop will be a contact, but very few contacts become people-links. Take the paint store owner, Carl, from Roger's story in Chapter Ten. Carl started as a contact. In fact, he was one of a number of managers and owners Roger initially met. But Carl became much more to Roger: his boss, former boss, a referral source, and a friend to boot. There should be many entries and lots of information for Carl-type links in any challenged seeker's database.

Roger didn't know Carl would become a people-link contact when they first met. You won't know in advance either, as you meet and enter people in your system. Don't worry about it; just get them in your database. Consider your system as a garden. Some seeds or contacts you plant will grow and others won't grow. A few will grow into huge, incredible plants. These are your people-links and there are only a few in each field.

A note from John

Setting up and maintaining your own information database won't appeal to everyone. It might seem like overkill or an unnecessary hassle to you, so you might decide to skip this step. Well don't. The approach presented in this book is based on meeting and connecting with people. You will need a system to keep track of those you meet. Keep in mind, however, by design my approach is targeted and not meant to be high volume. The return on your data entry investment will be significant, especially considering the length of time you will remain connected to many of your contacts.

Maintaining links

People-links are special. They're maintained through communication, and not just business-focused conversations. By the time someone becomes a people-link, you'll know a great deal about their lives, including personal facts about their family. There shouldn't be a month that goes by without at least one interaction with each link; a visit, a call, an email. Make it a point to remain close and top-of-mind with each link.

Keeping your links posted on the latest about what you're doing is critical to your success. If a people-link doesn't know what you're doing or working on, they're not really a good link, they're merely a contact. It's up to you to make sure they're up to speed on what's happening. Remember, if they're a true people-link, they will be interested in knowing.

Interacting and communicating with people-links isn't a one-way street. You may not be asked to do anything in particular by a people-link, but offer your help. They might be ahead of you in tenure and status, and they're probably fine with assisting you without expecting much in return. They get it; you're working your way in and up. Nonetheless, offer and be ready to be of service in any way you're able to help out.

Catherine Makes Her Big Move

A few days after Catherine told me about her trip to Kingman and her ex-husband's unexpected visit to her workplace, I called her boss, Roxanne. She answered on the second ring.

"Roxanne, hi. It's John. Good morning," The better I got to know Roxanne the more I liked her. She was unpretentious, open, fun, and she had a heart as big as Nevada. I was never sure what might come up each time I called her.

"Hey, John, how's everything in the job search world?" Before I could respond, I heard her yell to someone in the office, "No, not the green one, take the yellow ... right, the yellow one ... yeah, next to the rack." She was back on. "Hold on, John, I have to close my door." I heard her footsteps followed by the door closing. "Okay, sorry ... what's up?"

"The other day when Catherine and I met, she mentioned her ex-husband dropped by work. According to what she said there were no problems, I just wanted to get your take." Roxanne was more than Catherine's boss; she became a mentor to Catherine. The three of us shared a number of sessions together.

"He's been here twice, the time just before she met with you and once after that. You're right; there weren't any problems. The first time he told her he was moving to Wisconsin. Frankly, I don't think she believed him. The second time Robby came by to say goodbye. The ex is finally gone."

"Okay, well I guess that's a relief." One of those *Oh wow, things just dropped into place* thoughts popped into my mind.

"You'd think so, right? Especially with all she went through with the guy. But no, she seemed a little down about it. I don't quite get it, but relationships are complicated." She paused, "Did she tell you she finished her course at CSN last week? Two weeks early?"

"No ... I'm getting all kinds of new info this morning. It's good I called." I had an idea why she might've skipped telling me, so I asked Roxanne, "Is she avoiding the next step Roxanne?"

"Does a leopard have spots? You're damn right she's avoiding it. But we all talked about this, right?" We'd discussed it for close to two months. Catherine would finish school soon and the plan was to transition her away from Roxanne's business to a new job where her new network security certification and off-the-charts computer abilities could be utilized. Roxanne continued. "John, I've seen some of the scores and comments she's received from her CSN instructor. She could actually teach the class. Her teacher, his name is Jason, can't say enough good things about her. She blew through the material, and he let her test early. Apparently that's a first for his class."

So, there's the backdrop for my next meeting with Catherine. She finished the course, her ex has moved on, and now it was time to take the next and perhaps final step on her long journey. As usual, she arrived right on time. I shared my conversation with Roxanne as the opener to our meeting together.

As I spoke, Catherine sat for a long time without uttering a word. Finally, she took a deep breath and spoke slowly.

"I know, John, it's time to get moving. I'll never be able to use the certificate or do much with big networks if I keep working for Roxanne. But I like it there; you know that. Roxanne's like family. I guess with Robby leaving it seems like I should be ready to head into a whole new life even more. I mean, it should be good, but it's scary and hard." She conveyed this without much hesitation or emotion. It was as if she'd gone over it repeatedly before our meeting.

I let her statement hang in the air before responding. This was the moment I was waiting for, although I couldn't have described in advance just how it would show up.

"You ready to saddle up the pony and ride? We've got work to do," I smiled, but sat still. It was up to her now.

"Yes, I guess this is it, John. I'm ready to take the next step. It's funny, no amazing really, after the shelter, that warehouse job, you, Roxanne ... my CSN class. How does this happen, I mean come together like this?" she shook her head slowly, staring straight ahead.

Catherine's plan was to stay in Las Vegas, which posed a challenge. Companies with computer systems large enough to need someone with Catherine's certification and abilities weren't nearly as numerous as in metro areas like Phoenix or southern California. But she wanted to stay, so we devised a game plan to position her.

Catherine updated her JSO and asked her instructor for assistance with her résumé. Jason made sure it contained the critical keywords and had the right "tech" feel. He also coached her on the likely computer setup and IT department structure she'd encounter with the type of companies she was targeting. This turned out to be invaluable for Catherine. She also got business cards using the same font as her résumé and signed up for a free Insightly account. She did all this before starting her final CSN course. By the time she finished, she had thirty-five contacts loaded in her contact database.

Her search began again. Catherine went ahead and

- Posted her résumé on two online job-search sites

- Visited Nevada Job-Connect, the state employment agency

- Applied to three large hotel casino groups, and

- Made a list of non-gaming companies in the area matching her JSO

The online postings garnered a lot of interest mostly from recruiters who, in spite of her listing Las Vegas as her desired location, had positions available all over the country. She went on a couple of Las Vegas interviews set up by recruiters but nothing developed. Her visit to Job-Connect went fairly well, and she established a relationship with one rep, but many of the IT-related jobs available weren't in the area in which she trained.

Perhaps her biggest frustration came with the hotel casino jobs. In spite of good recommendations from her instructor, nothing developed. Catherine interviewed at all three and had a second interview with one, but the process ground to a halt. One group contacted her saying they selected another applicant. The other two just hung on with no real conclusion.

Catherine plowed ahead, working for Roxanne and following the first five steps of introduction, résumé, application, and two follow-ups with each potential opportunity. Every contact and every bit of information about them went into her database. She was approaching the six-week mark of her search when we met for lunch one afternoon at a café near Roxanne's office.

"You know, John, I'm wondering if not being a man in this field is an issue. What do you think?" She twisted two stirring sticks into a little glob of plastic as she spoke.

"Maybe, how many of the interviewers were men?"

"All of them except for some of the HR staffers. But every single one of the IT department personnel were men. I'm just saying; it looks like it might be a factor."

"What else have you noticed so far, about the whole process?" I wanted her take on things. From what I could see, she was doing everything right and putting in more than enough effort.

"There's nothing I can put my finger on. My background isn't a factor at this stage, at least I don't think so. I don't have a felony on my record, well you know that ... but, other than a few work-history related questions, nothing, really. I'm picky about my dress and manners, no issues there, I think."

Catherine kept me posted regularly. A week after our conversation at the café, she called to say she was excited because Jason lined up a meeting for her with a VP of Operations for a major beverage distributor expanding into Las Vegas. She went to the Bellagio Hotel to meet him for an interview. Typically low key, Catherine could hardly contain her excitement.

The morning after the meeting with the VP, I called her. She sounded down.

"What happened? Why so gloomy?"

"He didn't make it. The Las Vegas trip was canceled because of a problem in Milwaukee. He's not coming out here for a couple of months. I didn't find out until I was at the hotel!" Her words were coming far quicker than usual, and her voice was clipped and a little edgy. I had to admit, I liked hearing this side of her. "They aren't doing anything about the position until then. I learned he's in a management mastermind group that meets every few months, this time in Las Vegas. I happened to talk to another guy from Portland that belongs to the group. It sounds interesting."

I was saddened by the conversation with Catherine the day before, but excited by the call that came from her the next day.

"John, remember the guy I told you I talked with at the Bellagio? The one who belongs to the same mastermind group as the VP of Operations that canceled? Well, he called. Seriously, he wants to fly me up to Portland for an interview on Friday. They're expanding their call center in Vegas, and they need a network security person."

As they say, the rest is history. Catherine flew to Portland twice for interviews. She was hired as an assistant to the network administrator.

How to work contacts and links

Let's take a look at how Catherine managed her PTR to land her third job. First, she had four people-links when she started: me; Cora, her counselor; Roxanne; and Jason. By the time the Portland company hired her, she had plenty of contacts, ninety-six in all. Out of these she developed four more people-links: a recruiter, the representative at Job-Connect, an HR specialist in one of the hotel casino groups, and the Senior VP with the Portland firm. Catherine had eight people-links by the time she started her new job. These eight people and the other eighty-nine people in her database, are now part of her master contact list.

Catherine understood the importance of staying in touch with her links. Using her database information, she'll mix it up, a call here, an email or text there, and occasionally a visit or a meeting. She'll keep everyone abreast on what and how she's doing and she'll inquire about the same with each of them. In the meantime, she won't stop connecting. She knows the path to her current career and new life came to her via these links.

Now, back to how she did it. For starters, Catherine is the person who did the work. She had help, but she's the one who put the suggestions into action. She was willing to try which, for her, meant getting out of her comfort zone. I helped her with her Five-year Plan, in developing her JSOs, and I coached and guided her implementation at all the crucial stages.

Roxanne was her rock when she needed it. A successful businesswoman with a big heart and the ability to spot talent, Roxanne's role was to nurture Catherine and then kick her out of the nest and on up to the next level. In the meantime, Catherine happily produced three or four times beyond what she was paid because she felt safe, supported, and appreciated.

Jason was her mind-mate, basically two math geeks working and helping each other in the real world. He clearly saw Catherine's ability and wanted to assist her out of friendship and professional curiosity. He couldn't get over the fact that someone of her caliber had just walked into his classroom, seemingly out of the clear blue sky.

Catherine maintained these links with integrity. By that, I mean she did it in a consistent and conscientious manner. She followed through on what she started. Essentially, her links became her team, all working toward the same goal of helping her attain her next job.

You could say she was lucky to meet her next employer at the Bellagio, yet let me remind you she was there for a similar purpose, ready to introduce herself and interview with the VP who never showed up. Catherine made her own luck by being ready and on point. She was there on time, dressed, and prepped. She was ready to rock and roll; it just turned out to be with a different dance partner.

Catherine is now very much on track, in her career and her life. She is poised to return to school, advancing her AA degree and Certification to a Bachelor's degree and beyond. She's crazy good at what she does and finally with a good-sized, stable company; one that can provide a long-lasting career or be a stepping stone to a higher career objective. She's in a great place to continue her

PTR by joining a professional IT group or via business networking where she'll meet managers and "C" level executives.

I'll continue encouraging her to maintain her contact database, at last count a little over two hundred contacts and twelve people-links. This is Catherine's digital journal, of sorts, which is fitting given her personality and technical abilities. By the way, it all happened because Catherine stayed present, provided great service to her employers, and connected with other people.

Contacts and links belong to you

Your situation will be different from Catherine's. Still, like her, you'll need to connect with people and keep track of the information you accumulate, too. Don't let up. The minute you feel you can drop out and do it on your own, you're in trouble. The path forward is made much easier to navigate when you're willing to connect with people.

Consider the process of meeting people and developing contacts as a business function with a personal side. Everyone who assisted Catherine had both a business and personal relationship with her. She needed help. She needed to learn how to develop relationships and connections. Each of us was willing to assist because we liked her and saw her talent. As we helped, a bond of mutual trust developed. As the old saying goes,

> "All things being equal, people will do business with those people they know, like, and trust every time."

The same goes for making contacts and developing people-links. To be successful at building your connections you need to be willing to

- Get to know people and let them get to know you

- Make an effort to like people and be likeable as well

- Finally, trust people and be trustworthy toward them

You can say you're willing and have a nice system to keep track, but if you don't make the effort, you'll miss out on a grand scale. None of this has to be hard. It certainly doesn't require you be someone you aren't just to make an impression. The key is following the steps in an authentic, honest manner. Even without an exerted effort, you'll accumulate contacts and develop people-links. Do yourself a big favor and recognize this is happening. Make the effort and take the time to set up your own system of "trapping and tracking" contact information. If you're diligent about doing this, I guarantee you'll reap the benefits for years to come.

The Wrap-up

Glance back to the quotation about "know, like, and trust." Now, look at the first part of it, "all things being equal." The truth of the matter is that all things are rarely equal. You're operating at a competitive disadvantage, as you have a background problem. Therefore, you must take measures to level the playing field. Being likable helps flatten things out. Setting up a system to track and manage contacts and links is another measure.

Action Steps

Set up your database.

Take the time to input each contact.

Build people-links from your contacts, noting them as such in your database.

Chapter Twelve

Your Journey Forward

The approach introduced to you during the last eleven chapters has two primary objectives: first, to help you secure and retain a toehold in the Marketplace; and second, to show you how to effectively use and reuse what you have learned to reach your Five-year Goal.

How successful you'll be depends largely on your plan and your commitment to working your plan. This final chapter in "*Get Beyond Your Troubled Past*" expands on the important discussion about planning because it's where you'll begin once you finish reading.

Your Road Map to Success

The topic of planning has come up frequently throughout this book for a reason—it's essential. I'm sure you understand this by now. Importance aside, do you know and believe, I mean really **know deep down inside** that your Five-year Goal is achievable? You might believe it, or you might not believe it. I know that. I also know you may not be able to see yourself being bound or trapped by it. Perhaps you'd like to, but maybe your way has always been to keep your options open.

Here's a news flash: The chances you'll achieve your Five-year Goal by leaving your options open are zero. Zilch. Nada.

Here's more news: even if you stick to it, the goal you'll end up achieving will probably be different from the one you originally set out to accomplish. What? That's right, because there will always be something, big or little, that doesn't work out exactly as you planned. Here's the thing, there's no way to know in advance what that "something" will be for you, and it might turn out better than you thought.

So, don't hold back. Set your big goal thoughtfully, and go for it. Without a plan you can get lost and "keeping your options open" is a cop out. You know by now the Marketplace doesn't care about you or your plan. But if you asked it whether those with a plan do better than those without a plan, the Marketplace would fill you in fast. It would tell you that having a plan isn't enough. Those who do well, **work their plan**. They're dedicated, diligent, and persistent. The Marketplace would add that *it's up to you, of course*. Win or lose, achieve your goals or not, it's all the same to the Marketplace. But it's not the same to you.

As mentioned in the beginning of the book, I realize at first planning and setting goals may not come easy. Perhaps you've never done it or for some reason you decided it's not for you. I completely understand, because I see it all the time with my new clients. Nevertheless, my job is to tell you the truth and here it is: without a plan or road map to guide you, the odds are highly unlikely you'll reach your destination. Really high. Here are a few additional thoughts on why having a plan is in your best interest.

Your plan provides structure

Starting with your Five-year Goal and working backwards to four years, three, two, one, six months, one month, and next Tuesday, you get a **reverse road map** timeline. Where it stops is where you start, your initial JSO. You then flip that map back around and start your journey, mile marker by mile marker, until you reach your destination. Like any road trip, delays and detours are normal. When this happens, adjust. Find your way back to the main road and keep moving toward the next mile marker.

Your plan provides focus

Plans put action into context. You do what you do **because** you want to accomplish your goals. There will be times along the way when you'll ask yourself, "*Why am I doing this anyway?*" Or, "*Will I ever get past this step?*" Without a plan, you wouldn't even ask these questions. So, stick to your road map and get your vehicle pointed back on the main thoroughfare. You'll gradually get to the next mile marker and the one after that.

Your plan communicates

The effort and determination you put out sticking with your plan will be noticed by other people. Through your actions, brought about by proactive thinking, they'll begin seeing your plan as real. There's some powerful mojo afloat when this happens. You'll literally feel it, and it'll be like adding fuel to your tank, propelling your vehicle down the road.

You can talk all you want about what you intend to do, but sticking to your plan and "doing-the-do" always speaks louder than anything you say. In fact your "doing" is at the core of your integrity. I can't emphasize enough how important integrity is over time. Doing the right thing, in this case, sticking to and doing your plan, will become the foundation upon which you build your own road, a road that'll eventually transcend the barriers complicating your path.

Your plan and measurement

Your plan includes a timetable and a destination. You start at the beginning and end up at your finish line five years later. Consequently, your progress can be measured from the minute you start. At any point along the way you can judge for yourself how you're doing, making adjustments or course corrections necessary to stay on track and on schedule. Always remember, it's your plan and it's up to you to occasionally measure yourself and your progress. Don't expect someone to appear out of the Marketplace fog handing out progress reports. Be proactive and do the measuring yourself.

Your plan, recidivism and recovery

Most recidivism studies of ex-offenders end at three years. In effect, the three-year mark is an important target. If an ex-offender can stay trouble-free for three years after being released from prison, the chances of returning drop steadily. If you're an ex-offender and three years is a good marker, imagine the statistics for recidivism at five years? Staying on course for five years is exceptional. You'll have accomplished a few things and sent a strong message to everyone around you. Most importantly, you'll send a strong message to yourself, that you did it. Hitting your five-year mark both in terms of time and accomplishment is a huge deal and one truly worthy of kudos, congratulations, and high-fives.

For readers in recovery from addiction to drugs and alcohol, the five-year mark is in fact used by the Substance Abuse and Mental Health Service Administration in its definition of "recovery." Staying clean and sober for five years provides the dual goals of making it to the "official point" of recovery and achievement of your own vocational plan. Yet, as good as the five-year mark is, it doesn't eliminate or replace your Personal Job One to maintain your sobriety, whatever that looks like for you. Your PJO always comes first.

Your plan and work history

Of course your plan is far more than a road map. Stick with it and implement it properly, and you'll be like a big, asphalt machine laying down a whole new roadway. You're literally repaving your work history. Past gaps representing long stretches of old highway with gaps, cracks, and potholes remain but, month by month and year by year, they move farther back into your past. What used to be a red flag work history indicating "story attached," is now solid and consistent. What's more, there's a theme to it, your Five-year Goal and your current JSO.

Add it up for yourself:

Goal + JSO + Work History + People-Links = What?

It equals something other people, especially potential employers, understand. Your task is communicating it effectively. Delivering The Mail becomes easier and less of a stumbling block to get to the next level. You'll use what you've learned to present yourself to others as an aligned, congruent bundle of determination.

Your plan and references

What about references? If you've followed my approach, the only references you'll need to "come up with" are the ones used to secure your first job. All others will come from people-links developed in the course of working your plan. Don't worry, even your initial references will come from people-links, although you may not know them as such at the time.

Stop thinking of references in any terms other than people-links, because you have far more than "just a reference" with them. These are people who will literally carry water for you if you let them, but you won't. Always carry your own water while offering to carry theirs. You'll see for yourself just what a living, breathing, real live, three dimensional, people-link "reference" can mean to your career and working life.

As you prepare to search for your initial job, imagine how much easier it'll be to search for your second job about eighteen months later. The people-links you develop will produce references you'll use. Their willingness to recommend you and speak on your behalf are essential by-products of working your plan. Your work developing, nurturing, and maintaining relationship links can be seen in the same light as your work to earn a wage.

Aside from the worth and importance you assign them personally, these relationship links are flat out marketable, which means they're exchangeable for something of great value in the Marketplace. You earn them one by one and then you work to keep them. This is a secret many "employees" haven't discovered. But now you know. Don't ever forget it.

Your plan and outlasting negativity

Working your plan means doing something now that will benefit you later. This is best accomplished by staying present, doing your best as each moment gives way to the next. Moments add up. As with recidivism and recovery, time counts. The more distance and time you put between yourself and the bumps in your past, the better.

There's no cut and dried determination about how long it will take for the clouds to clear. Is it five years? Seven years? Ten years? It depends on a number of factors, but from my vantage point, things flatten significantly when you reach the five-year mark. However, let's not discount years one through four at all. Sticking with your plan gives you a chance to see what the journey itself has to offer beyond just the destination. Intangible rewards await at every mile marker. Like a mountain hiker, you must travel through the valley and up the slope to reach the next vista. Trust me, this is reason enough to buy into your plan.

Michael Falls Away from His Plan

Michael was late for our 11:00 am appointment. I tried his cell but, as usual, he didn't answer. Every time I left a message, he'd see I called and would call me back without listening to my message. I quit leaving messages for him a month earlier. I hung up and called Arnie's.

"Good morning, Arnie's, Randolph speaking, how can I help you?" I'd met Randolph a few times; he was animated and excitable.

"Hi, Randolph, this is John, I've been in a few times to see Michael. Can you transfer me back to the kitchen? I need to speak with him."

He was slow in responding.

"Ah, Mr. John, Michael ... ahhh … he doesn't work here anymore …." I could picture him grimacing as he spoke.

"What? Since when?" It just came out. I couldn't help it.

"Since Tuesday maybe. I don't know. I was off yesterday."

"What happened? Did he quit? Get fired? What?"

"He quit. That's what Orlando said. I don't really know. Sorry Mr. John."

This time I left a message on Michael's cell, to call me back ASAP. It took him three days to return the call.

"So what's going on with you?" It was hard to contain my irritation at the moment.

"I got a new job ... well, I'll have it soon. So I quit over at Arnie's." His tone of voice was flat and monotone.

"What do you mean 'will have soon?'" I could almost predict his answer.

"Well, I lined up a construction job ...." he replied.

"Construction? What company? Where's the job?"

"Man, what's with the twenty questions? I don't know. Mo's hookin' me up. I'll be starting at $14 an hour, with lots of overtime, too." His tone was pure street and 100 percent defensive.

"Okay, when do you start? Look, how else can I find out what's going on if I don't ask questions? When do you start?" I hated having to drag information out of him one sentence at a time, especially when he had his street armor and attitude on and locked in place.

"Sometime next week, I'm waiting for Mo to get back to me with the details." More street.

"Okay, Michael, if you want to talk it over, meet me somewhere or come to my office; I'm ready. What would you like?"

"I'm good, man, I'll get back to you after I start the new job. I'll let you know how it's going." No more street, back to the flat monotone again.

"All right, Michael, you know where to find me. Be safe."

I tried twice to connect with him over the next three weeks, but he didn't pick up or return my calls. I was ready to put him on the back burner when he finally called me back late on a Friday afternoon.

"So how's it going with the construction job?" I wasn't sure what to expect.

216

"It's not, I mean, I worked four days, didn't even get a full eight hours in on those days. It's a temporary job, man. Mo really screwed me over, man. Now everything's messed up." Blaming, playing the victim, little boy, street armor, all mixed together in his tone of voice.

"So what do you want, Michael?" I had to cut to the chase.

"I want my old job at Arnie's back. This construction job sucks man," he griped.

"Then get down there right now and talk with Orlando. He's usually there late on Fridays. If you want it back, do it right now and let me know how it turns out."

"I don't know, man ...." he said.

I cut him off.

"What are you going to do? Sit around and watch TV? What? Get off your butt and get down there if you really want it. Don't wait another second. Go!"

"Okay, I'll call you back later." Street armor dropped now, all little boy excitement.

I knew if he went, Orlando would ream him a new one.

Michael called me back later that evening. Orlando (the general manager) and Chef Thomas were both there when he showed up. Each of them bit a piece out of Michael's hide, but they took him back. Prior to suddenly taking off, he was one of the best prep-cooks Chef Thomas had ever hired. Michael provided good service; that was never a problem. Sticking with his plan was another matter entirely.

Michael's true dilemma

Michael had no difficulty doing the work at Arnie's. He was young, strong, and active. The continuous motion and busyness of working in a kitchen suited him perfectly. He learned quickly, made few errors, and he took direction well. That surprised me a bit, given his back story. Michael could do all this and, when he showed up for work, he was consistently "on." Chef Thomas appreciated this about Michael and brought it to my attention many times.

Working wasn't the problem. The issue that caused Michael to suddenly change course mid-stream was that he didn't identify with the work, being part of the team at Arnie's, or an ability to implement a plan on his own.

He identified with something else, the old crew including Mo and others. For Michael, going to work was like performing. He went from where he lived physically, mentally, and emotionally, to somewhere he didn't live. He plugged in and put on an excellent performance. Then he unplugged and went home. While at work, the show he put on was top notch and convincing. To others on the crew, Michael was terrific at what he did and a star performer in his role within Arnie's world.

In spite of a good show at work, the fact remained, Michael identified with the world where he was born and raised—where plans were merely dreams, relationships were bound by limits, and strict rules didn't easily transfer to other worlds. Yet, in spite of his strong identification, Michael didn't fully trust his world, either. Unfortunately, his trust for the world Arnie's represented was even less. The gravitational pull and comfort zone of his world eventually proved too strong, causing him to return. He was stuck and asleep, unable to see the Marketplace and couldn't care less. Michael was still in prison, not the one he was released from two years earlier with bars on the windows and doors, but the prison he lived in his entire life.

Michael's circumstances are a powerful reminder of the importance of making your Personal Job One (PJO) of utmost importance as you heal from your troubled past. It wasn't a lack of ability or raw intelligence that set Michael back. It was that he just didn't get his PJO. He heard the words, nodded his head in agreement, and could converse on the topic. But he didn't understand how profoundly his unaddressed PJO issues impacted his continued employability.

He got that the Marketplace would smack him good for quitting suddenly with no reasonable excuse. But he didn't fully understand why because he didn't identify with the rules of the Marketplace. Michael's PJO should have been to disconnect enough with his world to allow him to function in the Marketplace during working hours. But he couldn't see it. He was too deeply asleep and not fully present to the moment and his potential.

Sadly, a new JSO, an updated résumé, cards, positioning, all of it, went on hold for Michael. His challenges had deep roots, beyond the scope of what I could help him overcome. His issues are fundamental and structural ones, big challenges Michael needs help overcoming to even have a shot at achieving his goals and notching up to his potential. He can choose to wake up at any time, but the odds don't favor it. Instead, he may maneuver his way into sort of an odd "tweener-world," identifying with one world and partially identifying with another.

Even if he manages to find some in-between zone to live in, connecting with others and developing people-links will probably remain a troublesome area for Michael. As I've said many times throughout these pages, without people, background-challenged Michael and all the other "Michaels" out there must try to rely on paper and digits to navigate the Marketplace. It's not a pretty picture.

The Journey Continues

So it continues in life. Old behavior patterns play out, surfacing and resurfacing over and over until they don't any more. In a passage from her book "When Things Fall Apart," author and teacher Pema Chodron references a lesson applicable not only to each of us as individuals but also to the Marketplace where all of us must compete every day.

> "... we find that nothing ever goes away until it has taught us what we need to know. If we run a hundred miles an hour to the other side of the continent in order to get away from the obstacle, we find the very same problem waiting for us when we arrive. It just keeps returning with new names, forms, and manifestations until we learn whatever it has to teach us about where we are separating ourselves from reality ...."

Certainly, the words above are fitting ones to bring this book to a close. Perhaps the hardest thing to do is see things as they truly are and not as we perceive them. One reason we strive for our goals and dreams is to avoid the pitfalls built into doing things the way we've always done them while expecting a different result. Pushing ahead and staying on course almost guarantees that, at some point, we'll have to negotiate with ourselves about what's required to move forward successfully. Inevitably, something within us or about us will have to change along the way. In the process, we'll have an opportunity to learn some lesson that's eluded us up until that point in our lives.

Dig down deep and find the fortitude and courage within to stay the course. As you do, remain heads-up because once in a while it'll happen. A crack or fissure will appear in the usual, tangled clutter of the Marketplace. Suddenly, but only for a moment, there will be a clear line of sight. What is seen is written to the brain of the viewer, true vision. In one solitary snap of reality, how things really are, is imprinted in our consciousness. Then, it vanishes almost as quickly, as the shifting, changing sands of the Marketplace overtake and obscure the playing field again.

Vision of this sort is a reflection of our changing reality. In those moments of clarity, we find it amazing, even awe-inspiring. When acted upon forthrightly, that vision has a real shot of producing success, in spite of the mean old Marketplace. Perhaps some of what I offer is based upon the clarity of that vision, but I'll leave that up to you to decide.

I'd like to distill everything I've presented to you in the entire book down into three simple truths about achieving your career goals. Accept these truths and abide by them, and you'll do just fine.

The Three Truths

- The marketplace is what it is, dispassionate and unemotional

- A plan with clear objectives will guide your way

- It takes people and relationships to make it happen

Success comes to those willing to work in the present moment each and every day providing exceptional service, en route to achieving a big goal. My hope is you'll experience and believe in your own career vision as you work through this process. Regardless of the road you choose, always keep in mind that the journey is its own reward.

Travel Well.

John Jeffrey Lundell

Afterword

You must be wondering how everything turned out for our four clients. Here's the run-down on each.

Roger

The good news is that Roger's still employed by the paint distributor. The less than good news is that he stumbled and relapsed, again. Fortunately though, his employer provides a substantial benefit package including substance abuse treatment and counseling as part of their Employee Assistance Program. It's too early in the game to know what impact this will have on Roger's long-term tenure with his employer. However, in the short run, he missed an opportunity for a promotion due to poor attendance and less than stellar work performance, all related to his relapse.

In spite of a continued struggle with alcohol, Roger remains optimistic and thankful to have retained his job. There's little question Roger is capable and an excellent employee as long as he keeps his Personal Job One (PJO) front and center in his life. Time will tell for Roger.

Michael

Little has changed for Michael. He's still working at Arnie's, still living with his sister, and still trying to put the pieces together with his girlfriend, Victoria. Each time I stop by Arnie's, which I do quite often, I wonder if Michael will still be there. But there he is, in his chef's jacket and cap, buzzing around the kitchen, pumping out enthusiasm and talking a mile-a-minute with his co-workers. Occasionally, we'll chat and, for the most part, he seems content. In fact, during the last couple of months, he has taken on some line-cooking duties that have added to his skill set and his self-esteem.

I encourage Michael to stay the course at Arnie's, in spite of the fact that he's been there much longer than I usually recommend. But Michael hasn't yet come into full alignment and, as with Roger, time will tell for Michael. I must say however, I am cautiously optimistic. Arnie's has proven to be the right environment for Michael at this stage of his re-entry and career. Chef Thomas and General Manager Orlando, are people-links that will benefit Michael for many years to come, provided he stays on track.

Catherine

I don't see Catherine very often but she stays in close contact, calling or emailing every few weeks. She is extremely busy. Her employer is now paying for her to obtain her Bachelor's Degree from the University of Nevada Las Vegas and has made her part of a traveling troubleshooting team that works as needed on internal as well as client-based IT projects. Catherine is in seventh heaven with a job that couldn't fit her any better.

One impressive thing about Catherine isn't associated with her work; rather, it's the fact that she has maintained a consistent relationship with her counselor, Cora. Catherine's success came quickly, so much so in fact, I was concerned she could easily become overwhelmed. But, before I had an opportunity to discuss it with her, she called one afternoon saying she had switched from being a community health client to one of Cora's private practice clients. She'd beaten me to the punch. Catherine is very much in command of her own boat, charting a course far beyond anything either of us would have expected.

Walter

I checked in occasionally with Walter after his release from prison, sometimes calling, sometimes stopping by the Miracle Mile gallery. Walter's persona as an upscale art seller continued to progress. Each time I saw him he sported better suits, shoes, and accessories. Even so, his demeanor remained the same, a unique mix of gracious aloofness. It wasn't hard to see why he did so well as an art seller.

The last time I called the gallery, I found out he no longer worked there. I'd met the assistant manager, Rachel, a few times, so I asked to speak to her. She told me that Walter had given them a week's notice and had left. Rachel was in California during Walter's last few days prompting her to call his cell to say goodbye. It was disconnected. Walter just dropped off the radar.

I have no idea how everything is going for Walter. He didn't contact me either, and I suspect he never will. Walter bid his time, slowly but steadily putting the pieces together for his exit to somewhere else. I have to think he's doing just fine, on his own terms, wherever he is.

Final Thoughts

All four experienced success. Clearly, Catherine's achievement is easy to see, but Roger and Michael have accomplished a great deal too and both are still very much in the game. What they all share is engagement. In spite of setbacks, all were able to hold

225

their own and move ahead. Of the four, Walter implemented his plan in the most focused and deliberate fashion. Unlike Catherine, who experienced a dose of serendipitous good fortune, Walter meticulously inched forward in accordance with his plan.

I wish the very best for Roger, Michael, Catherine, Walter—and to you too. To each of you I say remain pointed straight into the wind, connected with other people, providing the best possible service at every turn.

Action Steps Summary

Listed below are the Action Steps found at the end of each chapter. I've expanded the explanation for each to add context and refresh underlying concepts. I encourage you to proceed step by step in the order presented.

Chapter 1: The Situation on the Ground

Visualize yourself as a Free Agent and not just an employee. More to the point, see yourself as a top notch, Free Agent employee, someone an employer would want to stretch to retain.

Imagine being an impartial third person observer, watching **you** in the Marketplace. What would you see?

Chapter 2: Waking Up to Reality

Identify your Personal Job One (PJO) and write out exactly what this means for you.

Practice getting and staying present. There's no cost or tools required and nothing to send away for. You came with what you need built in. Mindfulness, of which "presence" is only a part, is an entire field of study. Visit my website for additional suggested reading and resources on this and other subjects found in this book.

Chapter 3: Your Smartest Game Plan

Write out your Five-year Planning Goal in three parts. In five years you will be:

- Doing what job?

- Doing it where?

- Being what kind of person?

Create your Life Priorities List in collaboration with someone close.

Develop your Daily Action List based from your Life Priorities List.

Determine your initial Job Search Objective (JSO). This is an extremely important step! Remember, your JSO must align with your Plan (roadmap) and Goal (destination). Your JSO is where you start your journey.

Chapter 4: Early Action Required

Construct and implement your system to take care of old business. Resist the temptation to skip or get sloppy with this step.

Reflect on (and, if necessary, recalibrate) your attitude concerning The System. The angrier you get at doing this, the more you need it.

Chapter 5: Your Personal Starting Point

Determine your Personal Starting Point (PSP), the spot where you found yourself when the merry-go-round stopped. This is when you "awakened" to your true situation and what needed to be done in order to achieve your Five-year Goal.

Commit yourself to accepting the things you cannot change ... for now. Stating this in terms of being present, it means accepting what you must do in the here-and-now so you have an opportunity to do something different (and more to your benefit) later.

Dedicate yourself to truthfulness and honesty, because:

- It's the right thing to do, and

- It's in your best interest

See yourself as being in business for yourself from this day forward. Why? Because it's the truth—you are in business as a Free Agent.

Chapter 6: It's All About Communication

Practice being the receiver of your own message before you send it. Know that it's not what's intended that counts, but rather how it's received that matters.

Put into practice these four "get along" tips for any situation:

- Know the norms for a particular environment

- Observe how others act in different ways

- Mirror the positive behaviors you see around you

- Act or change or adapt your behavior to blend in

Review your social media presence. Apply the "less is more" rule. When you are re-entering the workforce (your initial JSO) you want **nothing** on the web that will detract from your face-to-face direct effort. There are exceptions, but they are rare. I repeat—rare.

Chapter 7: Setting Up for Success

Write and edit your personal narrative or story using the three-step method provided in this chapter. As with cleaning up old business, resist the temptation to skip or skim over this important step.

Conduct your own background check officially using state and federal sources.

Prepare your Ten-year List noting where you have lived (details) and what have you done (more details) over the last ten years.

Find and complete an application (big, detailed, and robust) that you can use as a template.

Create your simple and effective résumé using the five parts suggested. Keep in mind your résumé is a tool, not a work of art or grand historical document. Your initial re-entry résumé should be one page in length. Remember, your "job" is to achieve your initial JSO. As you advance and purposefully change employers, your résumé will evolve and grow. However, don't forget, you'll have people-links to help you. Avoid "fluffing and puffing" your résumé or yourself. Stay grounded, real, and pointed forward.

Chapter 8: Getting Your First Job

Use your narrative and create your Delivering The Mail or DTM statement. Boil it down to a few essential sentences to create your DTM statement.

Practice communicating your DTM, so it flows effortlessly as you say the words. Take this seriously, rehearsing with family and friends as if preparing for an onstage presentation.

Chapter 9: Retaining Your First Job

Maintain a journal for your first and every job. Add information daily or weekly (as it happens) concerning what you have learned,

230

observed, and experienced. From this, create your Discovery List, pulling out the big stuff and the highlights. You'll understand the value of doing this when it's time to update your résumé or get ready for interviews.

Prepare for your next job by taking the following steps:

- Create a new Job Search Objective

- Update your résumé

- Get business cards

- Tell your employer

Chapter 10: Positioning Yourself for JSO Success

Plan out the search for your second position using a Positioning Through Relationships (PTR) perspective and mindset. As you do this, make sure you

- Continue to supply stellar service for your current employer

- Foster key relationships at your first job (the source of your first people-links)

- Review your actual need for a social media presence:

  - If you don't really need it, don't do it

  - If you do need it, keep it tight, light, and narrowly focused

Chapter 11: Advancing Toward Your Goal

Set up your contact database.

Maintain your database. Initially this means entering each contact. You'll actually "use" this information later.

Thoughtfully yet deliberately, build people-links from the contacts you develop. People-links are critical to your success so "graduate" them in your database to a higher status deserving of additional detail and attention.

Chapter 12: Your Journey Forward

Create your Five-year Plan. Understand that it will

- Provide you with focus

- Communicate your intentions to others (and to you)

- Give you a way to measure your progress

- Help reduce recidivism and support recovery

- Produce your critically important work history

- Provide references in the form of people-links

- Establish positive forward movement

Beyond Your Troubled Past visit (www.getbeyonditall.com).

Coming out soon, *Get Beyond Your Troubled Past* **Workbook**.

About the Author

John Jeffrey Lundell is a Career Strategist and Relationship Trainer. He helps individuals and organizations achieve their objectives through strategic relationship building. His unique approach, as found in *Get Beyond Your Troubled Past*, incorporates mindfulness, self-awareness, sales principles, and personality theory. John lives and works in Las Vegas, Nevada.

www.getbeyonditall.com

johnjeffrey@getbeyonditall.com

Made in the USA
Charleston, SC
15 December 2016